WATCHING, WAITING, WALKING

*A pattern of prayer and
a path for disciples*

Andy Rider

First published in Great Britain in 2012

Society for Promoting Christian Knowledge
36 Causton Street
London SW1P 4ST
www.spckpublishing.co.uk

Copyright © Andy Rider 2012

SPCK does not necessarily endorse the individual views contained
in its publications.

Scripture quotations taken from the Holy Bible, New International Version
(Anglicized edition) are copyright © 1979, 1984, 2011 by Biblica (formerly
International Bible Society). Used by permission of Hodder & Stoughton Publishers,
an Hachette UK company. All rights reserved. 'NIV' is a registered trademark of
Biblica (formerly International Bible Society). UK trademark number 1448790.
Scripture quotations marked JB are taken from The Jerusalem Bible, published
and copyright © 1966, 1967 and 1968 by Darton, Longman & Todd Ltd and
Doubleday, a division of Random House, Inc., and used by permission.
Scripture quotations marked RSV are taken from the Revised Standard Version of
the Bible, copyright © 1946, 1952 and 1971 by the Division of Christian Education
of the National Council of the Churches of Christ in the USA. Used by permission.
All rights reserved.

British Library Cataloguing-in-Publication Data
A catalogue record for this book is available from the British Library

ISBN 978–0–281–06394–9
eBook ISBN 978–0–281–06978–1

Typeset by Graphicraft Limited, Hong Kong
First printed in Great Britain by Ashford Colour Press
Subsequently digitally printed in Great Britain

eBook by Graphicraft Limited, Hong Kong

Produced on paper from sustainable forests

For Carol, Rachel, Ben and Jacob

With thanks to Dad, Len, Gail, David and Scholastica, and the many others who have touched my life with their habits of holy living. Thank you.

Contents

———◦◦◆◦◦———

v

1

Heroes and habits

————••◆••————

Every morning that I wake up in my east London home I take a shower and choose a shirt to wear. This second task is often influenced by the plans I have for the day: pastoral visits, time with staff, city meetings, taking assembly in the school, walking the dog or clearing out dusty corners of our eighteenth-century church building. Some mornings I take time to sit with Jesus and contemplate the day with him, inviting him to speak into those plans. Now I am not a mathematician (although I am an accountancy tutor's son!) but I reckon that if I kept statistics then the days I add Jesus to the mix of shower, shirt and porridge are the days when I am more likely to have any sense that I might walk on the water instead of wading through the treacle of tests and trials that characterize our fast-moving complex city-centre life. I have learnt that when I take as long or longer with God in the morning as I do with some of the many daily tasks that fill my life as a church minister, I start the day with more peace than when I don't; however, there are days when, heading towards my personal 'place of prayer' and passing the computer, with its never-ending email inbox, unresolved internet searches and the piece of work left over from yesterday, I yield to temptation and am soon lost to a virtual world through my screen, rather than lost to a divine presence in wonder, love and praise.

I am in the second half of my life, and while I hope to grow wiser in the years that lie ahead, one thing I have learnt is that the world was not made for me or my ease. In fact, it wasn't made for a whole range of people and things that so often end up at the centre of our lives: celebrities, television, wealth, the internet or the family, to name just a few. No – I have learnt that the world was made for the carpenter's son who rose from the dead. It was made by Jesus and it was made for Jesus. 'For in him all things were created: things in heaven and on earth, visible and invisible, whether thrones or powers or rulers or authorities; all things have been created through him and for him' (Colossians 1.16). And that changes everything. At least it changes everything I used to think about me and the world and the shape of each day. It also seems to suggest that taking time with Jesus regularly may be a wise decision, a prudent investment of time. It may also help me to keep sight of the big picture, to gain a larger, wider, longer and higher view of things when the trials of everyday life threaten my peace and my perspective.

I live in Spitalfields, where the City of London meets the East End, where today the huge Bengali communities of east London and the new inhabitants of this vibrant neighbourhood rub shoulders on Brick Lane. Among the newer Spitalfields community are a number of artists, musicians, writers, producers and architects, people who are often referred to collectively as 'the creatives'. I like standing in the street outside my home talking to my architect neighbours in particular. I like their world of design and building. If you have ever marvelled at a bird in the sky, the power of a waterfall or the beauty of a sunrise, then you might just want to avail yourself of the opportunity that is always there to stand or sit with the 'eternal architect' who designed and brought the world to life. This book is about sitting with him, it's about walking down the road with him and it's about getting his perspective on our own lives. It's about seeking his peace in an ever faster, ever more stressful world. This book is essentially about developing habits within and around our Christian spirituality that shape us for tomorrow rather than trap us in yesterday.

I believe much of human life is composed of a series of habitual behaviour patterns; we are predisposed to habit-forming for the security and familiarity it gives us. When we face stress, pressure or tiredness, it is to our habits that we naturally return. I am exploring three habits in this book that I increasingly believe unlock a more fulfilling life of faith: three habits that, if we return to them often, will, even when we are under pressure, be a source of life rather than the exhausting trap that so many of our habits are; three pearls of great price that, once owned, should be polished rather than forgotten or hidden in a field. The three habits I am offering are each drawn from key moments in St Peter's life where he engages in a new behaviour or pattern. Peter: one of Jesus' inner crowd of disciples, who literally sat with Jesus often, walked with Jesus daily, heard his teaching and gradually came to know Jesus' perspective in his own life. Peter knew first hand and increasingly the peace of Christ in his daily life, a peace which, if we really knew it today, would transform not just our days but perhaps the world we inhabit.

Heroes . . .

Today more than ever, we live in the age of the celebrity – footballers, singers and stand-up comedians – a world where retired politicians can earn a fortune giving after-dinner speeches. All of us, like it or not, have been influenced by people we have heard of, read about or lived alongside. These people, whether worthy of celebrity status or not, can easily get under our skin and into our thought patterns without us even realizing it. They have the power to become our heroes, even at a subconscious level, and I believe this is happening more and more. We idolize them, and modern advertising often takes advantage of this inert human instinct. Most of us already have heroes: one of my earliest was my Sunday-school teacher with the red E-type Jaguar, later to be eclipsed by George Best and Ringo Starr! It was Len's car and his cool character that I admired. There was something else about him, though, which I couldn't quite comprehend at the time, nor could I, aged seven, have articulated it if I had realized what it was. I was nearing my twenties when I understood what made him stand out: he was a transformed man, one who lived in the daily conscious presence of God, inviting the Holy Spirit to visit him regularly; today I would say without hesitation that my Sunday-school teacher 'walked with God'.

Heroes have the power to influence us and draw our energy in certain directions, to shape our spending patterns and dress sense, or to pull our political opinion one way rather than another. A captivating sports teacher or musician may lead a young person to spend hours emulating that hero's skills, envying his or her success, or may even inspire someone to become a celebrity of tomorrow. You may love cooking wonderfully creative dishes and wonder where this passion came from; today's celebrity cooks have caused a generation to return to their kitchens, to buy fresh local ingredients and to spend a fortune on cookery equipment just to turn out a lasagne! Our film stars enable high street shops to sell fashion to the young as if it's going out of fashion! I want in this book to encourage us to open our eyes to who our heroes are and to deliberately seek out holy heroes – people like my Sunday-school teacher who walked with God. I want us to find role models who will influence, model and shape our Christian discipleship: godly people, people we would really like to be like when we are sitting with God. Have you ever paused to ask seriously who your heroes are, the people who affect what you wear and how you spend your money?

One hero of mine who stands out is Enoch, Enoch of Genesis 5, a truly holy hero. Little is known of him; Luke records that he was of the lineage of Jesus, just six generations away from Adam. His story in Genesis is extremely brief, just six verses from beginning to end; apart from his being a father who lived to the ripe old age of 365, all we know is that he 'walked with God'. It is the writer to the Hebrews who tells us a little more, namely that Enoch pleased God. Pleasing God is surely the primary endeavour of all Christian believers. If walking with God pleases God, then the holy heroes who will most help us are those who are themselves walking with God. Enoch, Simeon,

Mary and my Sunday school teacher each lived this life and inspired me. Many thousands of others have also walked with God and I have been blessed to walk alongside some of them. Enoch is one of my heroes not because of some mystical achievement but simply because he lived with God, day in and day out: he 'walked with him'.

A number of biblical characters are on my list of heroes, some barely known outside Christian circles and some misunderstood within them. Moses, Daniel, Sarah, Elijah, Jonah, Enoch, Simeon and Mary have become my role models; they have unknowingly helped to shape my spiritual disciplines and will appear from time to time in this book. Peter is one of the superstars for me. His life has humble beginnings, not unlike many of us; he doesn't enter the pages of history as anybody special, just a fisherman from a fishing family living and working in the Galilee region. However, from the moment he met with God in Jesus on his own familiar beach, his life changed. By today's standards many outside the Church will overlook him – he didn't set up a trust fund or start his own movement, and his writings may comprise just one letter, his authorship of 2 Peter being challenged in recent years. Despite all this, his name is given to many churches around the world, many of them famous. In the Church he is considered to be, after Jesus, the leading light; even though we have far more of Paul's writings it is Peter whom Jesus charges with founding the Church, and who is considered by the Catholic Church as being the first Bishop of Rome.

It is in the Gospels and the Acts of the Apostles where we find the real Peter, with stories both mundane and amazing recounting his life in the unfolding Jesus story. Jesus, the carpenter's son, later the risen Lord Jesus, chose Peter to be a close special friend; he called Peter to follow him and he challenged Peter to grow into the person God intended him to be. Peter did just that. Today Jesus wants to impact us, that in our ordinariness we might be changed, transformed into the men and women God intends us to be. The question for each of us is: how will we co-operate with God's will and pursue godliness amid the distractions, temptations and aspirations that are modelled to us by our more immediate heroes, idols and celebrities? By intentionally choosing the right heroes and considering their lives, we may be more inspired for the life of faith; by looking at Peter and developing the holy habits that can be perceived in his life, we will find ourselves walking more closely with God and will be spiritually transformed and readied for all that he has in store for us.

Peter

It takes Peter a long time to understand Jesus, but from their first contact Peter is attracted to the wandering rabbi. Jesus is Peter's hero, and Peter allows Jesus to shape him so that at the end he has learnt to walk with God. In the early days he intuitively realizes that Jesus holds the key to his own life and maybe the key to the lives of many others. This Galilean fisherman, interrupted one day while fishing with his brother, becomes through the immediate incarnate ministry of Jesus a leader of the early church. Today Peter might have been a postman, a teacher, a musician or a web designer, and 'Peter, I will make you a fisher of men' would be 'Peter, I will make you a courier of God', for this simple artisan is chosen by Jesus to go and shape people's lives, to convey the good news of Jesus to many. He becomes in fact a shepherd as much as a fisherman, a preacher, a pastor and an apostle. The point is that he starts out an ordinary guy, someone like you and me, simply surprised by the person and teaching of Jesus.

Peter may well have been regular in prayer before meeting Jesus, but we are not told that. He may have been faithfully seeking to please God, but we are not told that. What we are told is that Peter's life is radically changed by Jesus: he is trained, moulded, challenged, rebuked, encouraged and ultimately transformed from bumbling over-enthusiastic fisherman to saintly pastor and apostle of the new church. The good news is that Jesus wants something of that for each of us: to live fuller, richer, deeper lives, to live out what we were made for, regardless of where we are when we let Jesus find us. Whatever our occupation, relationships or personality traits, Jesus will have more in store for us; he came that we might have life to the full. As Augustine says, whatever our mistakes, failings or weaknesses, 'Jesus is at no loss to perform his will concerning us.' He can – and, if we let him, will – transform us by his grace, his words and the power of the Holy Spirit. The challenge so often is: how do we let him do that? And how do we keep letting him do it?

Peter makes a decision when he first meets Jesus: to follow him. It is a decision that is critical to the direction of his whole life. A little while later, when Jesus asks him, 'Who do people say I am?' Peter replies, 'You are the Messiah' (Matthew 16), uttering a statement explosive among the rabbis of the day, politically pinning his colours to the mast of the new man in town. In response Jesus gives him a new name: 'From now on, Simon Peter, you will be known as Cephas, "The Rock".' In the same tradition whereby Abram became Abraham, Sarai became Sarah and later Saul would become Paul, the name change symbolizes a moment when a line has been crossed and Peter's very identity is renewed; through time spent with Jesus he is already becoming a new creation.

His mortal life ends, we are told by Origen, when he decides in Rome to be crucified upside down, not worthy to die the same death as his Saviour. Between deciding to follow Jesus and his last mortal decision, Peter will face a number of significant moments and subsequent choices. Three moments in particular, where Peter has to choose whether or not to live the way Jesus has set out for him, will change him for ever. These three moments form the key 'lessons' for Peter that will shape his spirituality such that he becomes someone who walks with God.

The first of these three moments in Peter's life occurs the night before Jesus is crucified. All our eyes are drawn to the action of Good Friday, and rightly so, but in Gethsemane, the night before he dies, Jesus calls Peter to 'watch and pray'. Peter and many others have learnt that spiritual watching is vital to living the Christian life; it is the foundational choice we each have to make as we set out to follow Jesus. And it will feature often in the life of the intentional believer.

The second critical moment I am considering occurs as the Eastertide drama unfolds. Following the death and Resurrection of Jesus, the story moves to the Mount of Ascension; as they ascend the slopes Jesus calls Peter again to make a decision that will change his life and the life of the Church more than any other. Peter and the disciples are asked very clearly to 'wait' for the Holy Spirit before doing anything. Peter again chooses well in the moment, and his obedience leads to both the birth of the Church and our second 'holy habit'.

The third critical moment for Peter takes place in Jerusalem itself, just outside the Temple, the spiritual centre for God's people till this point in history. It is a moment, a choice, a decision that Peter has unknowingly rehearsed. Some months before, Peter responded to another of Jesus' invitations, the one to walk on water (Matthew 14). Often this little story is tucked away in Sunday-school memories, but for some it is an inspiring story of faith and focus, keeping our eyes on Jesus amid the tumult of everyday life. For Peter it was a preparation for a life of faith as he lowered himself over the gunwale of the boat, with the first rays of dawn in the sky, and walked upon the waves towards his Master. It was a prophetic act, as he would one day step out in faith and begin walking daily with God in trust and surrender, no longer just following the God-Man from Nazareth but walking with him. Which leads us to the third moment in Peter's life that evokes a spiritual discipline, when, on the day of Pentecost, he steps out in faith, stepping out into the world – with as much faith as he stepped on to the water – to address the jeering crowd. It marks a turning point in his personal life and will be the springboard for the fledgling Church. Peter will a few days later complete this step of faith when he bends down to invite a crippled man to stand and join him walking fully and faithfully with God.

Peter has led me to see that these three holy habits of watching, waiting and walking really can transform a person's life. They each – and, more importantly, together – hold the key to how we might fan into flame the gift of the Spirit which is in us (2 Timothy 1.6) that we might in greater trust live out our days pleasing God, as did Peter, Simeon and Enoch.

Habits . . .

So this little book is about habits. It is about intentionally developing habits that will help to shape our spirituality. My early mornings are filled with habitual behaviour, from coffee-making to shirt-choosing, from tidying the kitchen to listening to the radio. Habits form us: 'What we do with our days we do with our lives.'[1] We each become the fruit of our habits. For a while in my previous church we were joined from time to time by an international marathon athlete. I remember him telling me he could eat almost whatever he liked, for the simple reason that his running schedule, his training habits, had such an impact on his body that his metabolism was quite unlike that of the regular person in the street. Imagine how it would be if your spiritual habits had such an impact on you that you were unlike the person in the street and more like 'the person at the right-hand side of God'! Those who habitually play sport become fit, those who habitually rehearse music become musical, and those who habitually shop become captivated by materialism. Those who are regular in Sunday worship become the Church, and among them are those who habitually pray and sit with God – they will become more like him, as they spend time in his presence.

If by reflecting together on Peter we can develop some habits that transform and shape our lives into greater patterns of godliness, then this book will not have been in vain. Over the years many have sought to set down habits for the Christian life, from scribbled ideas in a journal to full-blown 'spiritual rules'. The earliest rule set down for a Christian community was probably written by Pachomius in the 300s and led to the founding of the Cenobite order.[2] Since then, rules have been crafted by many: Basil, Francis, General Booth, the Taizé community, to name some of the most well known. My personal favourite is the Abbot of Monte Cassino. Benedict of Nursia wrote his rule for the religious houses he founded in Italy. Today Benedictine communities can be found the world over and his rule is often considered the benchmark of monastic rules. All these patterns and rules seek to develop in the adherent habits for daily living that keep alive in us the desire for God that first gripped us, habits and holy desires that respond to his grace and goodness. Maybe you already have a rule of your own; a good friend of mine lived for years by his: 'to pray daily, fast weekly, retreat annually and seek to show God's love continually'.

St Benedict wrote in the introduction to his rule, 'We hope we shall lay down nothing that is harsh or hard to bear.'[3] Many of us have a tendency, especially when setting ourselves towards discipleship maturity, to burden ourselves with great long lists of disciplines, as if by creating complicated plans we will make holiness easier to accomplish. Actually the opposite is true. Holiness is simple: it emerges within our lives as we turn them over to God and allow his Spirit to transform us from inside out. The hard part is that our human tendency is part of our fallen state and we habitually rebel against God. I hope the patterns of formation and prayer here are simple, not harsh or hard to bear. The hard bit is always choosing to go God's way.

I hope that as we explore three key moments in Peter's journey and as we consider how they may become our own habits, we will discover refreshment and invigoration in them that will shape us. I believe these three holy habits, practised daily and dwelt upon within the rhythms of our own lives, will help us to walk more continually with God, pleasing him just as Simeon, Mary, Peter and Enoch did.

What we do with our days – we do with our lives.

2

Watching – the Gethsemane habit

———•—•—•———

[After the meal] Jesus went with his disciples to a place called Gethsemane, and he said to them, 'Sit here while I go over there and pray.' He took Peter and the two sons of Zebedee along with him, and he began to be sorrowful and troubled. Then he said to them, 'My soul is overwhelmed with sorrow to the point of death. Stay here and keep watch with me.'

Going a little farther, he fell with his face to the ground and prayed, 'My Father, if it is possible, may this cup be taken from me. Yet not as I will, but as you will.'

Then he returned to his disciples and found them sleeping. 'Couldn't you men keep watch with me for one hour?' he asked Peter. 'Watch and pray so that you will not fall into temptation. The spirit is willing, but the flesh is weak.'   (Matthew 26.36–41)

'Watch and pray'

> More than all else, keep watch over your heart,
> since here are the wellsprings of life.
> (Proverbs 4.23, JB)

The first of the three 'moments' in Peter's life that I am considering is in many ways the most inauspicious. It happens in the dark of night, and it presents itself as a moment of failure for Peter. While it is true that we learn from our mistakes, and indeed this is what I believe happens for Peter, it is in many ways sad that the mistake then has to follow Peter all his days and for centuries after his death. Maybe that is what a life well lived involves: learning from our mistakes and in humility

11

living with them unashamed to share the learning with others. The story involves Peter, Jesus and just two other disciples, so it is reasonable to assume that in some way Peter was party to the sharing of this story. It is a story of failure, of being overcome by darkness within and around, for it is in the dead of night that Jesus finds Peter asleep and it is this 'sleeping on the job' for which Peter becomes known. But it is Jesus' response to Peter's drowsiness that brings about lasting change in Peter's life and that will form our first discipline.

Peter's relationship with Jesus was at risk through his failure to follow a simple request from his teacher. Jesus had become not just a teacher to Peter but a close personal friend, and his request was neither hard nor complicated. Peter was not asked to stand on his head or complete a Sudoku puzzle as Jesus prayed: he simply had to stay awake. Peter had spent many evenings with Jesus; it had been a long journey to Jerusalem, staying in various people's homes along the way, and this particular evening had been the feast of the Passover. Peter had eaten well and drunk a few glasses of wine. He, James and John had been chosen especially to accompany Jesus, to *walk with Jesus* further into the depth of the olive grove so that Jesus could withdraw from the crowd. It was now late in the night and the darkness, combined with the warm smell of the olive grove, would cause many to relax. It is not uncommon for someone's eyes to grow heavy while sitting at the supper table late at night with friends; it is easy to imagine Peter and his fellow disciples struggling to stay awake late into a Mediterranean night. For even when the spirit is willing, the flesh is often weak.

Jesus finds Peter asleep. He knows his heart, that Peter wants to follow him, to be his number two, to receive divine blessing, but he also knows that though Peter is convicted of his aspirations, putting them into practice is a struggle: perseverance does not always come easily. Jesus is right, 'the flesh is weak'. Our search for holy discipline has to overcome our own temporal weaknesses. Perhaps this is best captured by Paul when he writes,

'I do not do the good I want to do, but the evil I do not want to do – this I keep on doing' (Romans 7.19). It is the old humanity, the unregenerate me, the part of me that needs God's transformative hand, that so often holds back the me of hope, faith, trust, peace and promise. Jesus offers the remedy as he offers the diagnosis: 'watch and pray'.

While in the dark night Jesus is awake (recall the psalmist, 'God neither slumbers nor sleeps'), praying for himself and for us as tears of anguish drop from his brow, sorrow overwhelms him and the horrors of tomorrow beset his lonely mind, we all too often fall asleep. Jesus declares to the sleepy, guilt-ridden Peter, 'I know your spirit is willing but not resolute enough to overcome your earthly weaknesses.' It is the same today; it is perhaps the single most significant reason why the Church in the West is floundering. It's why Paul writes to the young Ephesian church, 'Wake up, sleeper, rise from the dead, and Christ will shine on you' (Ephesians 5.14). It's why the transformed Peter begins his letter to the dispersed Christian community,

> With minds that are alert and fully sober, set your hope on the grace to be brought to you when Jesus Christ is revealed at his coming. As obedient children, do not conform to the evil desires you had when you lived in ignorance. But just as he who called you is holy, so be holy in all you do; for it is written: 'Be holy, because I am holy.' (1 Peter 1.13–16)

The Church ever since has too often been found slumbering and unprepared. Peter learnt the first habit, to watch and pray, to be alert, remaining sober and avoiding sleepiness in his intention to follow Jesus, and we today also need to learn this habit if we are to be holy as he is holy.

The first discipline to adopt into our daily pattern is the discipline of watching. For many of us, Jesus' words resonate too readily with our struggle to remain awake and watchful. Peter in the Gethsemane narrative doesn't choose not to watch with Jesus – it is rather more subtle than that. He simply chooses not to choose. He submits his decision-making faculties to the weariness of his body, the weightiness of his soul and the worries of the world. Today we may call it stress, anxiety or even exhaustion – it is the pressures of modern-day living that simply tire us, and they rob us of the riches of God's grace. Time and again we choose not to choose; distracted or exhausted by modern living, we submit to this world, to old ways and to old habits, rather than to Christ. Jesus, when he calls Peter to 'watch and pray', is calling Peter to make a choice, to choose a spiritual discipline that will work in him God's purposes to perform.

Watching is the habit, while watching and praying is the fuller expression of Jesus' word that night. After looking at how we 'watch', we will consider how we might start to 'watch and pray'.

Why is watching important?

What I say to you, I say to everyone: 'Watch!'.
(Mark 13.37)

I love walking along the beach; I enjoy walking the streets of central London; I get satisfaction from walking through the royal parks; and more than anything I am most often myself when walking in the mountains. In each of these places, watching where you walk is vital: oil lumps on the beach, broken kerbs in the city, dog detritus in our parks or loose rocks on the mountainside. Caution is wise.

I was walking in the Welsh countryside. We were on a family holiday staying with friends near Carmarthen, and like most young boys the last thing I needed was to be hanging out with my folks so I wandered on ahead with my brother. Before long the voices of the others had faded and we were alone. It was an area of mixed woodland, the sun filtering through between the big deciduous leaves one minute and hidden by close conifers the next. I cannot recall now what led us to separate, but we did and I was soon by myself. I have always loved being alone with nature: the sights, sounds and smells of the countryside are a simultaneous source of comfort and exhilaration.

That day in Wales I was at one with the world – woods in particular lend me a sense of well-being – when all of a sudden I was falling. Not falling over, simply shooting downwards. I grabbed for whatever I could find. Nothing seemed to hold me as a handful of earth came away, and then a clump of grass, but as it did so my foot seemed to find something firm and moments later I was standing on the smallest of ledges pressed against a cliff like a mountain face, unable to go up or down. I was far enough down that for some 20 minutes or so my calls for help went unheard while my family, alerted by my brother, had at least begun to wonder where I was. Eventually I was discovered, and with the help of a rope and much encourage-ment I clambered safely back up the cliff to the waiting crowd. And then my father broke into one of his annoying songs, 'Mind where you put your feet'.

Even now, re-telling the story, I can recall the feel and smell of earth and rock and grass in close proximity to my face as I slid down the cliff. I can recall the relief at being found, and the words of that song come back to me, complete with tune! I am not sure the song was originally composed for country walks but its lyrics remain appropriate, both to walking in the country and to the desire to walk with God.

Minding where we put our feet is vital for safety and can change for ever the joy of a walk in the countryside. The spiri-tual discipline of watching is in part about avoiding falling into the many traps along the way that threaten to derail our life of faith.

When toddlers begin to walk they will have been watching experts for a year or so and want to be like them. As they start to totter they will soon learn to watch their own feet in order to keep safe. As Peter begins learning how to walk with God, he watches Jesus, keen to emulate his inner stillness and his intimacy with God the Father. Jesus teaches Peter not just to watch his example but to watch over his own life, to turn his life over to prayer, to be mindful of God in his daily life and choices. The habit of 'watching' will call each of us to imitate Jesus and to mind ourselves if we are serious about walking faithfully with God.

Watching

Watch your life and doctrine closely.
(1 Timothy 4.16)

What Jesus is saying to Peter in the garden of Gethsemane is that he must take care of himself and his attitudes if he wants to be a faithful disciple and an example to others. Watch yourself, watch out, be careful. In the garden Peter's sleepiness meant that he could not do what he wanted to do: he was unable to stand by his friend and Master in his hour of need. Where else would he fail in the future if he didn't learn to take care now? Thankfully for Peter and for the Church and the mission of God, Peter did learn to watch and pray. We need to be watchful too.

I believe that when Jesus told Peter to watch, he wanted Peter to watch him, to see an obedient, faithful, servant-hearted life in action. I am human and have been for a long time – I think I have a rough idea how humans work, and we are at heart selfish. So much of our lives are 'me'-centred. I remember as a young Christian being taught to shape my prayer life around the acrostic ACTS: adoration, confession, thanksgiving, supplication. It sounds great, but the truth is that to adore another or to thank another requires my putting the other first, while to confess means recognizing that I am not right: only in supplication can we remain at the centre of our world, as it is so often for ourselves that we *supplicate*. Prayer teaching needs to start with an introduction to the concept that at the very heart of a praying life is a need to put God at the centre and to step back and off the pedestal we so often climb upon. Life is messy;

we need to acknowledge our self-interest and then we can work with the mess. Instead of inadvertently worshipping ourselves we are to watch ourselves, taking care over who we are and the opinions we form of ourselves. In this way we can open ourselves up to real God-centred prayerfulness, and it is this that will begin to transform us.

Watching ourselves can be this first step towards prayer. There are two parts to watching ourselves and Paul spells this out when he writes to Timothy. He decides to encourage the young Timothy, urging him to tackle heresy, help the church seek propriety during worship, and assist with the appointment of elders and deacons in the Ephesian church. Then, before turning to more practical aspects of the church's faith and teaching, Paul has some words for Timothy himself because he so wants Timothy to please God and to stay spiritually on track. Paul knew that godly leaders are first godly disciples and he may also have known the words of Jesus in the garden of Gethsemane; perhaps they were told to him one evening over supper. Perhaps Peter's walk with God had inspired Paul and he had himself learnt to 'watch and pray'.

Paul urges Timothy to be diligent in his discipleship, and he says, for the benefit of us all, 'Watch your life and doctrine closely. Persevere in them, because if you do, you will save both yourself and your hearers' (1 Timothy 4.16). These simple but profound words of exhortation echo and expand the Gethsemane words to Peter. They offer such wisdom to all who would follow Jesus that I want them to shape my own discipline of 'watching'. Our first holy habit takes its shape not just from the garden but also from the daily grind of living spiritually in a pagan society. Watching ourselves, we must learn to watch our life *and* our doctrine.

Watching your life

My father grew up in Brighton, one of two boys in a relatively poor single-parent family, his mother taking jobs she wasn't qualified for in hotels and restaurants where tips were enhanced by stolen food and crockery! She did well by her boys, and Dad studied to better himself while working full-time and bringing up his own family. As a result he had little time for 'spongers', convinced that the government during the 1970s was creating a welfare nation of over-dependent families. He, like many of his generation, became suspicious of the increasing levels of energy exerted by the state to assist individuals to do what he felt they could be doing for themselves. By the 1980s and the dawn of the counselling revolution he had run out of energy to fight, but continued to question the new middle-class fascination with therapy and social welfare, which now extended far beyond the initial intentions of Beveridge. My dad predicted that the welfare state, instead of addressing idleness, was encouraging it.

He had to struggle with a son who for a while was in social work and peddling self-awareness courses, first in psychiatric day centres and then in children's homes. Today many management techniques, therapies, relational training and communication skills are based on good levels of self-awareness. Regarded by the older generation as unnecessary and ultimately a form of selfishness, introspection has found a firm place within modern society. I believe it can lead to unhealthy levels of self-absorption, but it is not all bad. Harnessed for God it has a right place within our holy habits. Simply put, if I self-reflect for my own personal gain and health it will quickly feed the errant selfishness which lurks within me, but if by reflecting honestly on my life I am enabled to move beyond my self-interest to better love God and neighbour, it is of real value to me and to the growing work of God's kingdom. Truly confessional living requires us to regularly self-reflect as we watch over our lives.

Most of us know the fleeting pleasure of being overcome by temptation. If we are honest we know too the lasting disappointment it often brings, and many have discovered the longer-lasting damage it can leave on our physical, emotional, relational and spiritual well-being. Even in daily life we quickly become aware of how easy it is to order a large glass of wine when all we really wanted was a small one, or to choose to stay in bed longer than is sensible with the list of chores we have diligently set ourselves for the weekend. Of course, many of our decisions and actions are much more significant and can have a lasting impact on our lives and the lives of others. If we are serious about wanting to walk with God, we will need to regularly address the disappointments, damage and scars that we bring upon ourselves, otherwise we will at best only limp with God. Be assured he is not unhappy with those who can only limp with him, but he wants so much more for each of us: he wants us to live as Enoch did. It is this deep desire for more that leads Jesus to urge Peter to watch and pray, and Paul to urge Timothy to watch his life and doctrine. God is already watching over us, lest our feet slip; he watches over city and field; he is the good shepherd, who loves and cares for his own, and he invites us to participate with him in shepherding ourselves and any in our field of care.

There is a practice which rightly forms a good habit for watching over one's life that many have discovered to be helpful over the years. Found within various Christian traditions, it is most commonly referred to as the examen, a spiritual exercise whereby the individual spends time quietly at the end of the day open to God, reflecting on what has been and allowing memories of the day to surface in order to be healed, redeemed or simply confessed to God. Depending on our own spiritual upbringing, this habit of confession will look different for each of us, but for all of us there are elements which are crucial. One is giving time to it, time that is quiet and unhurried, for there is much to be done, far more than we ever imagine. This watching over our life is essentially about learning to live confessional lives, aware that we have fallen short of God's glorious intentions, but aware too that by bringing our lives into his grace we receive his forgiveness and live in his righteousness.

Living confessionally is at its heart simple, for there is much help at hand. The Bible is probably going to provide the bedrock of our habit of watching over ourselves, for it is there that God reveals what it is that he hates about humanity. He discloses those attitudes and activities that disappoint him, those we should rightly be ashamed of and in which we ought to seek transformation. Galatians 5 has for a long time been a chapter to reflect upon in preparation for making a sacramental confession. But so too the Sermon on the Mount, where Jesus unpacks the law and warns those who would be his followers about the life they are to leave behind.

The Holy Spirit also helps us. He is eager to lead us into all truth, and will gently bring to mind those things that we have done, and those things which we have failed to do, that need to be brought before God as we attempt to step out of the old patterns and into the new life. He will bring to mind the careless and hurtful word uttered in the busy workplace or the unresolved difficulty with a close relative, those faces and names that we have offended or neglected. But we have to give him time, and we mustn't rush madly at the first thought that occurs to us or alternatively become obsessed by it, as there may be more. Once we have opened our hearts to let the Holy Spirit search us, Jesus' promise of forgiveness is realized in our hearts.

'Let us draw near to God with a sincere heart and with the full assurance that faith brings, having our hearts sprinkled to cleanse us from a guilty conscience' (Hebrews 10.22) and let us do it often. For, needless to say, if we only ever have these times of reflection annually when on retreat, there may be so much that comes to mind that we drown in our own disappointment. Those traditions in the Church that encourage a weekly confession in worship are assisting with the health of the Church greatly. Those who take time each day to reflect on their lives and to confess to God their shortcomings will in fact be enriched and enabled to overcome those very shortcomings. For, to be sure, no healthy person eats just once a week, or cleans their teeth once in seven days, and God is always ready to receive us. 'Praise be to . . . God . . . who daily bears our burdens' (Psalm 68.19).

We cannot live out our Christian faith simply by watching over ourselves. Our faith is not about self-help and personal development, nor is it about a moral life – it is about living godly lives. Romans 12 speaks of us being transformed from one degree of glory to another, but that will require us to have a clear vision of what glorious lives look like; if our desire is to be more like Christ then we will need to be constantly refreshed in our understanding of who Christ is and what our life in him is to be like. It is this Paul wants Timothy to gain by watching over his doctrine.

And watching your doctrine

Doctrine has never been the preserve of theological students or those at Bible college: it is simply the word used by the Church to describe the body of 'Christian teaching', so to watch over our doctrine is to be intentional in our learning about God and the Christian faith. When was the last time you stopped and asked yourself, 'What is it I believe?' or considered the orthodoxy of your Christian faith or how what you believe relates to the world of ethics or work? When was the last time you recited a credal statement outside of Sunday worship? I have a sneaky suspicion it may be some while ago – perhaps you can't even remember. Yet we are daily beset by the underlying beliefs and values of the media and society leaders. How do we respond? Are we equipped for entering the debate by the photocopier from a truly Christian perspective? If not, we are leaving ourselves vulnerable to views that are at odds with our own declared faith. It will not be long before syncretistic belief patterns rage within our soul. This is not simply a concern that secular liberalism will begin to influence the Church, though that does concern me; it is more a concern that to live a life of faith we need to know what we are putting our faith in. And that requires us to have some clear ideas about the depth, beauty and reality of our relationship with Jesus.

The oldest story in the Jewish and Christian traditions tells of how Eve, left alone for a while in the Garden of Eden, encounters a snake, the personification of evil, and how he lies to her about God and his purposes. As a result of the lies that lodge in her mind Eve makes a huge mistake, and Adam follows her unquestioningly into it. This story continues to be played out day after day all around the world. Many of us know what it is to be misled by a third party, to form wrong opinions and develop wrong ideas about those who are important to us. Truth is perverted and authenticity is lost. At a personal level this can be a disaster and can wreck relationships. In the journey of faith the original story is still being played out: lies still have the power to get under our skin and into our minds to such an extent that our view and understanding of God becomes perverted and disconnected with reality. Here too it will lead to a broken relationship and we will lose sight of God and lose touch with his reality.

On one occasion some years back I attended an evangelism training session where we were each asked to write down what the gospel was for us. My own attempt in those few short minutes was:

> The gospel is that no matter what you have done to this point, God's love is undiminished towards you. The death and Resurrection of his one and only Son is effective in bringing you to the fullness of human expression in his Spirit and in his kingdom, now and in the hereafter. Furthermore, he invites you to co-operate with him in renewing the face of the earth.

I have no doubt a wiser theologian would in the same few moments have come up with a far better summary, but I was quietly pleased with myself. However, my pleasure turned quickly to disappointment when I saw the struggle of many on the course to put down anything much at all, and realized that those who did were not at all confident of what they had written. Many of us are not really very sure of our doctrine at all.

A friend I enjoyed working with for ten years would from time to time remind younger members of staff that they should always 'be ready in season and out' to give an explanation of the gospel in three or four easily memorable phrases. He spoke often of his four planks of the gospel: the creation, the fall, the rescue and the return. I have for many years, as a result of his encouragement, turned to three Bible verses as a summary of the Christian faith: '[God] has ... set eternity in the human heart; yet no one can fathom what God has done from beginning to end' (Ecclesiastes 3.11), 'Come to me, all you who are weary and burdened, and I will give you rest' (Matthew 11.28) and 'For to me, to live is Christ and to die is gain' (Philippians 1.21). I will often read them through in the morning as a springboard for the day, adding, 'So let my soul live that I may praise you, and let your word be my sustenance' (Psalm 119.175, my wording). The simple act of recollecting these verses each morning helps me start the day intentionally rooted in a biblical understanding of the world. It also helps me to meet the people and challenges of the day with a more divine perspective.

In his book *Sit, Walk, Stand*, Watchman Nee tells why he starts with the sitting position. He says, 'Christianity does not begin with walking; it begins with sitting ... For Christianity begins not with a big DO, but with a big DONE.'[4] He wants us to stop and realize the significance of Jesus' sacrificial death and its impact on our lives. His argument is completely right: we cannot begin to walk with God if we haven't first grasped who he is, what he has done and how we can rest in his salvific peace. Watching over our doctrine will not only bring us to the assurance of peace, it will also ready us to live our days in the power of the Resurrection and to walk in the constant presence of God's Spirit.

A better way to understand the word 'disciple' is that it means not so much a follower of Jesus but a 'learner', after the teaching and pattern of Jesus. Most of us, in order to follow, need to attend to our deficiencies in learning; we need to sit with Jesus more than we do and learn more of who he is and what he is about. In the simple practice of reading the Scriptures, we will most often grapple with what God wants us to know of him, for this is where he self-reveals. Some have found the practice of *lectio divina*, 'divine reading', to be helpful; originating from the Carmelite and Ignatian traditions, this describes a way of reading God's word so that our own agenda becomes subject to his will through the reading of the Bible. There are four simple steps: *lectio*, where we read the Bible slowly, letting it sink into us; *meditatio*, where we ponder the text and reflect on it, asking what it might say to us; *oratio*, our response, where setting aside our thought processes we simply respond from our hearts to God. The final stage is *contemplatio*, where we rest, letting our plans, worries, thoughts and ideas slip away while we rest in the word of God, listening at a deep level to God's (often still, small) voice. Many have found this the most effective way to live daily in the light of God's word, to be transformed by his truth.

In the business of watching over our doctrine we are rich in resources: study aids, Bible commentaries, Christian study days, conferences, teaching holidays and courses. With the internet and now computer tablets and Kindles, it has never been easier to read, and there are some great Christian writers around that are available to us. We could do a lot worse than to read some of the more historic Christian fathers and mothers of our faith, who have stood the test of time and provided substantial pillars of Christian wisdom. But perhaps one of the best places to begin the discipline of reading in order to watch over our doctrine is with the classic credal statements the Church has written to define its doctrine. It will assure you of your orthodoxy, and prepare you for those moments when you are asked to define or defend the gospel. I would suggest sitting quietly with the Nicene Creed, pondering the phrases, praying the truth contained within it. A slow reading of it will open our minds to God's redeeming love and serve to close the gap on our drifting doctrinal standing.

On the edge of the inside of the pulpit in All Souls' Church, Langham Place, is inscribed, 'Sir, we would like to see Jesus', part of John 12.21. Each time I preached in that church the words would catch my eye. They were meant to – they were put there to challenge each and every preacher that we preach Jesus Christ and him alone. But the words came when 'There were some Greeks among those who went up to worship at the festival. They came to Philip . . . with a request. "Sir," they said, "we would like to see Jesus."' These visitors to the region wanted to know him more fully, to see and hear him in action, to meet with him if at all possible. Today we want to know him more fully, we want to know he is there and we want to meet with him often. Just like those Greeks, we will need to take time and to ask others and to go looking for him. The psalmist had it right when he said, 'One thing I ask from the LORD, this only do I seek: that I may dwell in the house of the LORD all the days of my life, to gaze on the beauty of the LORD' (Psalm 27.4); he would be echoed years later in the life of Mary, the sister of the over-anxious and busy Martha. Perhaps for us gazing upon God's beauty is something of a metaphor for watching our doctrine, because in studying God we will often find worship arising within us.

Watching and praying

> Hear my cry for help, my King and my God,
> for to you I pray.
>
> (Psalm 5.2)

Jesus tells Peter to watch, to be alert and aware of the sin that can so easily beset him, because Jesus wants Peter to resist evil, to watch his thoughts, words and actions, to exercise spiritual self-control. Jesus would also encourage Peter to watch 'holy role models'. Peter was a Jew and would look back to Abraham, Moses and Elijah; he would remember the faithful among his ancestry and now he had the ultimate role model in Jesus. As we watch over our doctrine we are simultaneously watching Jesus, the cornerstone and focus of our doctrine. No wonder it is said that 'good theology always leads to good worship'. It has often been said that Anglican theology is found in the Anglican prayer book, just as Methodist theology will be found in the Methodist hymnal. It is inevitable that if we truly study God we will come close to him, and will want to reach out to that which is the subject of our attention. Watching our lives and our doctrine will lead us into prayer and worship.

Our quest is to develop habits that help us follow Jesus, so looking to him will be vital; Peter discovered this when he tried walking on water. How can we follow someone if our eyes are not trained on him or her? If we want to walk with God but have not begun to talk with him, it will be an impoverished and unsatisfying walk. In the closing scenes of the Gospel, Peter doesn't seem to have learnt the art of watching over himself very well but we do see his eyes fixed on Jesus. He follows him to the courtyard and to the cross, he runs to see him on Sunday morning and he jumps into the sea when he sees him on the beach. This hunger for Jesus will not always be there for us. It will dry up if we do not take time to fan the flame of faith or to rest in his truth. We need to cultivate our relationship, and we need to take time to know the person with whom we want to be in relationship.

While many of us appreciate the value of self-awareness, fewer of us put such weight on what I call 'other awareness', an intentional pattern of behaviour that will bring us into greater awareness of those we meet and spend time with, to be present to them to the point of hearing, seeing and perceiving who they really are and what they are really about. Today many of us live at breakneck speed, barely living in the moment, so that when we are with a work colleague our minds are actually somewhere else, or when we are making idle conversation on the bus we are quite disconnected, busily planning in our head for the weekend. To cultivate 'other awareness' will be a fundamental skill in building community or offering pastoral care, and it is also a vital tool in building a life of prayer. It is the ability to intuit God's presence in the room. A friend had a sign on his door so that he could see it whenever he left his college room: it read, 'Slow down, you move too fast, you can't see your brother when he is walking past.' This 'other awareness' is what we need to cultivate in our times of prayer.

Prayer for many of us has become squeezed out, or pushed into little time slots so that we can race around doing things that seem more urgent or important. While this whole book is about catching the daily essence of God's presence, it is here in the second aspect of the habit of watching that I believe we find a nugget, a pearl of great price; it is here that I want unashamedly to encourage you to put Jesus on the top of the tree, to watch him and to reach out to him. I want to redis-cover 'prayer for prayer's sake' – not simply the liturgical routine of confession, intercession, supplication and thanksgiving, but adoration and engagement, prayer that is rooted in both the self-knowledge that comes through watching our lives and the divine awareness that comes from getting our doctrine right. Prayer that grows out of these foundations will be significantly different from the prayer routines and the prayer lists that so many of us are weary of.

Just pray

Prayer, even for the most mature of believers, rarely begins with-out something of a decision. It can occur without a pre-thought as it catches us unawares, but I have yet to meet someone whose prayer life is rich and fulfilling if it is based simply on random moments of unplanned (emergency) prayer. Prayer, as with any form of communication, begins with the desire and the deci-sion to make contact; prayer begins with the will. It takes a decision to pick up the phone or write a letter, and even texting and emailing are based on a desire to connect with someone. For so many of us this is where prayer fails; it is said that the greatest point of spiritual vulnerability is the moment between waking up and getting out of bed. In these moments, when we choose to pray or not to pray, when we decide how to start the day, the battle for a prayer life is won or lost. When in sleepiness we lazily make the wrong decision about how to start the day, we so often lose the whole day – and we are far the poorer for it. Finding special places, times and patterns will help us in our prayer but they are, in the words of David Runcorn, mere scaffolding.[5] If I light a candle in my familiar place of prayer and assume a posture that has helped in the past, if I use some familiar liturgy and meditate on a Bible passage, I have lots of scaffolding, but unless I intentionally engage with God during prayer I am simply exercising an absent presence. If a spirit of prayer is absent, if a desire to reach out to Jesus is not within me, then no amount of scaffolding will build a life of prayer. Where does this desire get nurtured? It is on a Sunday, in a mid-week group, through reading or attending a conference, it is in the attention we pay to doctrine, in the time we give to 'learning' of Jesus, for it is as learners that we are most fully his disciples.

As we see, consider and know again Jesus' grace, beauty, luminosity, power and generosity, we will naturally want to reach out to him from our shallow world of shadows. When, that balmy night, Jesus said, 'Watch and pray,' he wanted Peter to watch over himself but also to watch over his understanding of God, to lean into the divinity and power of God, for the strength to stand up to the world and the assaults it would make on him. Peter was being told to call upon God for the strength to resist temptation, to beseech God to guide him from darkness and death and into light and truth. Prayer is the activity of trusting God and leaning not on our own under-standing or strength (Proverbs 3.5); it will be rooted in our knowledge of him and his purposes.

I often remind myself and others in leadership that it is those who make themselves most available to God who will find God making himself most available to them. But it is not always that simple. Often, people tell me that God seems far away and it is true, I think, that not only do we move away from him, knowingly and unknowingly, but sometimes he seems to withdraw a little from us. Much has been written about wilderness spirituality. For many of us there will be very real and lonely wilderness times along the way. My concern, however, is that we don't inadvertently walk into one which God would not have us in. The first step towards an unhealthy wilderness experience can be as simple as a week without drawing near to God; it can be a 'staying away' from church and Christian friends, right at the point of our deepest need. While it is certainly not always the case, sadly it does often seem that diminishing times of intentional prayer mark the road into the desert, until the road is indistinguishable from the surrounding land and the way-markers have disappeared altogether. Prayer is rarely an accident, and we cannot wait for the accidents to happen; we have to direct our will towards wanting times of authentic prayer.

The monastery bell has called me to prayer when I am on retreat; it continues to inspire me when I am not. I might be wandering through the monastery gardens, asleep on the bed in the guest room or reading in the library, but the bell that chimes me out of whatever I am doing and calls me to the chapel to pray is the reminder to my inner being that I do actually desire to walk with God. It prompts me to decide, there and then, to stop whatever I am doing and join the others who are also intentionally drawing near to God and discovering in doing so that he is drawing near to us (James 4.8).

The same Peter who is told that, having watched, he is to get on and pray, later writes 'the eyes of the Lord are on the righteous and his ears are attentive to their prayer' (1 Peter 3.12), for whatever his own pattern of intentional prayer he has learnt and wants to pass on that the life which includes a habit of prayer is the life that is watched over by God himself. Peter's prayer routines were rooted in his Jewish upbringing; today, the *Daily Prayer Book* of the synagogue still provides not only for morning, afternoon and evening synagogue services but also for private prayers to be said on rising in the morning and retiring to rest at night. The pattern of Daniel when he is in Babylon is reflected: three times a day he intentionally gets down on his knees to face Jerusalem, prayer shaping his daily life. Prayer for Peter and his contemporaries would be largely focused around the psalms, reciting the various names of God, remembering aloud the stories of God among his people. It was to some extent where doctrine was done, but it was also where communion with God was entered into. Jesus himself teaches Peter and his friends to pray, introducing them to what we know as the Lord's Prayer, a pattern of adoration, intercession and confession. A healthy habit of daily prayer will involve set times and, best if more than once a day, it will include time in the Bible, in and out of the psalms and the Gospels in particular. It was here that the Celtic monks went to meet most intimately with God and is the reason they taught their protégés to recite the psalms and Gospels from memory. A healthy daily habit will only be blessed if it includes the Lord's Prayer. It will only ever happen when we decide to take time for it: 90 per cent of prayer is the intention to pray, when the will is aligned with God's, when the eyes of our heart are gazing into heaven, seeking out the Maker of the universe, his comfort, peace and direction.

Living confessionally

This habit of watching our life and doctrine and being led into prayer and praise is best described as 'living confessionally', for at its heart it is about knowing me and knowing God. It is in confessing who we are and our genuine need of God that we live most fully. It is the crux of a life built on God, and unless we return regularly to this habit of 'watching' I seriously doubt whether we will ever grow in our faith. I would fully expect Christians who are not engaged with this habit personally as well as with others to find their faith running dry. Why did Jesus say to Peter, 'Watch and pray'? Because he knew that if Peter failed at this first discipline of transformation he would fail at every subsequent one.

Let me encourage you to develop the habit of watching over yourself, watching over your doctrine and turning both into the prayer of confession, admitting to God your true condition and deeply considering again who Jesus really is. Confessing who I know myself to be and who God is will be the bedrock of any Christian journey, and it is always the first step in walking with God.

> Holiness comes from Christ. It is the result of vital
> union with Him.
>
> (J. C. Ryle)

3

Waiting – the Bethany habit

After his suffering, [Jesus] presented himself to them and gave many convincing proofs that he was alive. He appeared to them over a period of forty days and spoke about the kingdom of God. On one occasion, while he was eating with them, he gave them this command: 'Do not leave Jerusalem, but wait for the gift my Father promised, which you have heard me speak about. For John baptized with water, but in a few days you will be baptized with the Holy Spirit.' Then they gathered round him and asked him, 'Lord, are you at this time going to restore the kingdom to Israel?' He said to them: 'It is not for you to know the times or dates the Father has set by his own authority. But you will receive power when the Holy Spirit comes on you; and you will be my witnesses in Jerusalem, and in all Judea and Samaria, and to the ends of the earth.'

After he said this, he was taken up before their very eyes, and a cloud hid him from their sight.

They were looking intently up into the sky as he was going, when suddenly two men dressed in white stood beside them. 'Men of Galilee,' they said, 'why do you stand here looking into the sky? This same Jesus, who has been taken from you into heaven, will come back in the same way you have seen him go into heaven.'

Then the apostles returned to Jerusalem from the hill called the Mount of Olives, a Sabbath day's walk from the city.

(Acts 1.3–12)

'Wait for the gift'

As for me, I watch in hope for the LORD;
I wait for God my Saviour; my God will hear me.
(Micah 7.7)

The second habit on our journey of discipleship is the habit of waiting. It doesn't come easily to most twenty-first-century Westerners, and it didn't come easily for Peter either. Again and again we see him rushing in where angels fear to tread. Leaping out of the boat ahead of the others, Peter walks to Jesus on the waves. John tells us it is Peter, in the garden, who reaches for his sword to attack the Roman soldiers. Following the Resurrection it is Peter again who leaps out of the boat and splashes through the waves towards Jesus on the beach, leaving his friends to pull the boat in by themselves. And moments later Peter rushes to assure Jesus that he is ready to be the leader of the Church, the pioneer and pastor of the new and fragile Christian community. Three times Jesus asks him if he is sure about taking on this commission; Jesus remembers Peter's previous hasty confidence that came to nothing. Peter remembers too, particularly the bonfire outside Caiaphas' courtroom that awful morning that Jesus was crucified.

I can remember many times committing in the heat of the moment to visit someone, or to work on a talk, or to help someone with a chore, yet when the time came my enthusiasm waned. Peter, of course, had agreed to stand by the Son of God to follow him wherever, and here he was again, committing. Would it be different now? Had he learnt to watch and pray so that his faith might strengthen him to overcome his weak resolve and to live out the eagerly made commitment? Peter is afforded the chance to redeem his three denials with three positive responses, and by so doing he is readied for so much more that God has in store for him.

A few days later, the beach breakfast has blurred into 40 days of meals with the risen Jesus. Peter is growing in confidence; he has been alongside Jesus in some large rallies – over 500 had turned up on one day. Now they are again with Jesus, eating and drinking, but today there is a strange atmosphere in the air and Jesus is not quite himself. They have been to the Mount of Olives hundreds of times. This time it is quiet – no crowds, just Jesus and his closest friends – and yet it feels shaky. Jesus seems to finish eating before the rest of them; wiping his lips, he looks at Peter. A kind smile, but something is not quite right: is a question coming? Peter will never know what lay behind those eyes, because they have wandered on around the Eleven, then out among the women and the young ones that are with them. Peter stops eating, a question nagging him: what was that look about? Just at that moment Jesus speaks: 'Do not leave the city. Wait for the gift I promised you.' Peter loses a breath, his heart misses a beat. Maybe the time has come. He has somehow known it would. But was it meant to be like this? With Jesus nothing is ever the way it was meant to be.

I believe that whatever happened that day, whether it was on the Galilean slopes as Matthew recalls or the Mount of Olives as Luke records, Jesus would most certainly have given Peter a knowing look or a gentle touch. So much was at stake; this man had emerged throughout the last three years as the one on whom he wanted to place his mantle. Elisha had wanted a double portion of Elijah's spirit; Solomon had asked God for the gift of discernment to rest in his heart; Peter seemed to think he could do it in his own strength, yet even with this flaw Jesus knew he was the one. So he had called him, and then he had called him Peter. He had invested in him extra questions, special visions and privileged opportunities. Jesus knew full well that Peter had much to learn: patience, self-control, faithfulness and how to be quiet within. The Holy Spirit would help bring these qualities to Peter – they would be first fruits! But Peter would need to develop these qualities himself. The Spirit would also equip Peter for the task ahead and begin completing him to be the leader he was born to be.

The disciples left the Mount of Olives and went back into Jerusalem. Without their rabbi and Master, life would be very different. Jesus had seemed certain this was not the end, and he had spoken before of the promised gift. He had taught them that a Spirit would come upon them in time, and it would lead them into deeper truth about him, and fit them to live without him. He had taught that this Spirit would be as him to them for the rest of their lives.

The ten most important days in the life of the Church are the ten that begin on the Mount of Olives, with the command to wait in the city until the promised gift arrives. Today we have all been frustrated when the delivery company cannot give us a fixed time between 8 a.m. and 6 p.m. With Jesus there was not even a definite day at this stage: just wait a few days, be still, remain. It was unequivocal, so final and absolute that there really was a very simple choice between obedience and rebellion. There is often a very simple choice between obedience and rebellion, but we tend to complicate things in an attempt to find a middle way, to make the decision easier. The Christian life, like the life of prayer, is not easy but hard. On the other hand, it is quite simple despite our constant attempts to make it complicated; if we would give up making it complicated and hoping to make it easy, we might just find the hard path rather simpler than we imagined. Peter and the other disciples have begun to learn this 'Jesus way': they make a simple choice and choose the hard wait. For ten days they wait in the upper room in Jerusalem. Acts 1 gives just 14 verses to the record of this waiting season, a season that reflects so many in the history of God's people: seasons of waiting for children, for freedom, for answers, for mercy and now waiting for the gift. Eleven disciples, the mother and brothers of Jesus and 120 others simply choose to wait.

It is in the waiting that Peter and his companions are being formed and made ready for the next chapter of their lives. It is in the waiting that we see the real leadership qualities of Peter emerge as he takes charge of the group and arranges the election of Matthias to be the twelfth disciple, replacing Judas. The key aspect of Peter's formation is the very fact that he is discovering patience: he is learning to incorporate the practice of waiting into his life.

Nothing has changed. Today many of us, like Peter, want to do it in our own strength – we are quite unlike Elisha. Not many of us beseech God for wisdom as Solomon did; too many of us are wired to live our lives alone, and even church leaders too often seek to exercise their ministry in a rushed and busy manner without leaning on God. Waiting is too often absent from our contemporary lives: we have replaced patience with anxiety and stillness with agitation, resulting in lives that are arguably more pressurized and stressed than ever. Can we explore the discipline of waiting? Waiting for the gift of the Holy Spirit to come upon us today?

Why is waiting important?

We will never find time and no human has ever
actually made time; all we can ever do in this
regard is to take time.

Peter was told to 'watch' in Gethsemane, a place of pressure where the olives were pressed to produce fine olive oil. Peter was over-burdened that night and was further pressed to watch over himself daily and to pray the teachings of his Saviour; watching Jesus, he would grow into his own identity and ministry. Luke records that it is Bethany where Peter and the others are told to 'wait' and it is from Bethany that Jesus ascends to the Father's right hand. Bethany was where Jesus often retired to rest while he was ministering in Jerusalem (Matthew 21). He stayed once at the home of Simon the Leper, where a woman visited and poured expensive nard over his head (Mark 14), and at the home of Mary and Martha, where he commended Mary for sitting at his feet, the better way, while Martha busied herself and got anxious (Luke 10). It should not surprise us that Jesus chose this place to tell the disciples that their next work would be the work of waiting, because sitting, resting and generous anointing are all divine characteristics that don't come naturally to most of us. Both Micah (4.4) and Zechariah (3.10) speak of a final day when we shall all sit under our fig tree and have fellowship together. Bethany typifies this sense of stillness and 'being' in God. Jesus tells them to 'tarry a while'; this will be where they and we learn to rest in God, pausing with Jesus, receiving forgiveness, grace and the Spirit – in short, learning to be dependent on God.

In a small way I was to learn this aspect of dependency, the ability to relinquish, the day I found myself quite literally waiting around in St Bartholomew's Hospital. I had gone for some minor day surgery and stood outside the ward door with the other 30 or so patients, nervously waiting to be let in at 6.45 a.m. for a trip to the seat-less theatre. The door finally opened 25 minutes late and I was ushered through to a cubicle and given a gown. Moments later I was having my blood pressure checked, and a pre-op conversation with the doctor followed shortly after. I will confess to being impressed that by 8.15 I was processed and just waiting for the porter to take me along to theatre.

I was less impressed when I was still waiting eight hours later, dry from no fluids since the night before, bored with the *Metro* newspaper and frustrated that on this one occasion I had abandoned my normal practice of taking too much reading matter with me. In the task of waiting we have to find a deeper patience within ourselves or we will go mad. With all the thinking time I had had that day, I realized as never before the huge trust that was being called forth from me as the needle went into the back of my hand and I was asked to count to ten. I realized I was completely entrusting my body, my very life, into the hands of the anaesthetist. I would have no control whatsoever over when and if I came out of the anaesthetic. That day, in the waiting, with the choice between patience and pointless madness, and in the ante-theatre, I met a moment of complete surrender. Needless to say, because my operation was so late they kept me in overnight, and I had even more time to reflect on waiting.

Another occasion was during 2009 when I was travelling overland from London to Istanbul – car, coaches, trains and a ferry! I had just taken the overnight ferry from Bari in southern Italy to Igoumenitsa on the north-west coast of mainland Greece, where I was hoping to find a coach to begin my journey east. I was planning to stop for a couple of days in Kalambaka to see the monasteries of Meteora. None of these places had I been to before and I don't speak Greek. As one of only a very few passengers to disembark at Igoumenitsa, I found my way to the bus station and introduced myself to a very Greek receptionist with few perceptible social skills, even less English and not much interest in customers like me from out of town! Still, I finally prised out of him the information that there would be a bus that day to Kalambaka, but he couldn't or wouldn't say when. Then he miraculously managed to convey to me that I had at least an hour to wait so should visit his nephew's café a few streets away for breakfast!

The sun came up, breakfast was good and I wandered back to the bus station just on the hour. No, the bus had not yet left, I was assured, but people had emerged from nowhere in the meantime and the place was buzzing with passengers, luggage and even livestock in the form of chickens. Buses seemed to be coming and going quite steadily. Yes, there would definitely be a bus to Kalambaka that day but no one could tell me at what time. So the waiting began, with little information and the smallest waiting room imaginable. I waited outside in the hot sun, something that would become a feature of my bus journey across Greece. I realized that each bus put the name of its destination in the window as the people were boarding, and since the buses left moments later the chance of missing mine was high. Eventually at about 3 p.m. a bus put up the name Kalambaka and I rushed over to join the queue. Those in front of me were in the wrong queue, so I was first to board the 52-seater bus. We didn't leave straight away, like all the other buses, but sat there for a further 40 minutes before the driver and I pulled away in an otherwise empty bus for a two and a half hour journey. I guess they had simply been waiting for more passengers. I had learnt to have faith – faith in the Greek receptionist, the Greek bus service and the fact that I would eventually reach my destination. I was in no rush, as I had a week to cross Greece, but as I reflect on it now it seems like a metaphor for waiting on God, waiting for someone else to make things happen. Peter, in waiting for the gift the Father promised, would wait faithfully in Jerusalem for ten days, looking to someone else to make things happen, patiently and faithfully surrendering the rest of his life to his heavenly Father.

Waiting

My soul finds rest in God; my salvation comes from him.
(Psalm 62.1)

After watching over our lives and our doctrine and taking time to meet with God in prayer, we ourselves must learn to wait upon him. It is the pattern of the Church and we do this because he invites us to; the psalmists respond to God that they are regularly waiting on him as well as singing to him – indeed, they very often sing about their waiting! With Peter, Jesus' invitation has even more direction, for it is God's will that he should wait in the city. It is Peter's choice whether or not to obey the words of Jesus and wait as requested, but it is clearly God's will that Peter should not try to take the good news to the world before, first, waiting on him and, second, receiving the Holy Spirit. God is not about to simply bless Peter with the Spirit; there are lessons to learn before Peter will be granted the powers of heaven to live the life he has been made for. Perhaps this is an echo of the master's words in the parable of the talents: 'Well done, good and faithful servant! You have been faithful with a few things; I will put you in charge of many things. Come and share your master's happiness!' (Matthew 25.23). If Peter can be good in the simple command to wait, God will increase his prospects; if Peter can be faithful to God through the long days and nights of waiting, he will be put in charge of much more and granted the Father's happiness, the Father's Spirit with which to go forward. If Peter leans into God in obedience, he will find God always leans graciously towards us.

Following the Resurrection there is a night when Peter goes fishing. Has his patience run dry? Nothing seems to be happening so he returns to familiar ways. The days between Jesus' Ascension and the feast day of Pentecost were completely different: now Peter is learning to look to God, to wait upon him in obedience. It is this habit which I want to develop and I invite you to do so too. It is not easy, as it requires us to relinquish other habits – habits of being busy, being in control, responding to our anxieties, worrying about what others might think, habits that take our time and zap our energy. I have often entered the room in our house where I like to sit with God in prayerful attentiveness only to be drawn instead to the desk, with its tireless cry for attention. Others speak to me of how the habit of getting up at the last minute before going to work robs them of the precious moments they might otherwise have spent 'waiting on God'; instead, arrow prayers on the tube is all that he will get. The prayer of waiting, the task of sitting with God, seems so passive that we often cut it short to tidy the room or wash the dishes, habitually (or is it obsessively?) tending to the trivial and missing out on the eternal. It will involve us in stopping, drawing aside from these other ways of being, resisting the temporal pulls and the ever-present opportunities for instant gratification. If we don't often get round to watching over our lives and doctrine, the simple habit of waiting on God will seem even further away.

God has lessons he wants Peter to learn, and it will be through the discipline of waiting that Peter will develop these attributes. God has done the same with Abraham, Moses and Elijah; he has done it with Sarah and with Mary; he has caused Israel herself to wait upon him that her people might look more readily towards him. I love the Christmas stories of Simeon and Anna, both quietly waiting in the Temple precincts: with their obedient, disciplined lives carved out of the practice of waiting, they each get to see and to recognize the baby Jesus ahead of the rest of the world.

Rembrandt's *Simeon* (well, a copy, actually!) hangs above my desk, calling to me to wait more often than I do. The old man's eyes are nearly closed, the beard is grown long, the clothes merge with the shadowy background of the Temple, and so in a way does Simeon: his own life is not his focus. He lives to see the Son of God; his focus is God's coming, and he is ready to meet him, for then he can say, 'Lord, now lettest thou thy servant depart in peace, for mine eyes have seen thy salvation.' Peter is such a young tempestuous man in comparison, pushed and pulled by the pressures of daily living. He will learn the three oldest lessons in the waiting time: he will have to be patient, he will need to draw from the depths of his faith and he will discover the inner stillness that is depicted in Rembrandt's *Simeon* and found in countless disciples and pilgrims who have learnt this habit of quiet patient waiting.

Waiting cultivates patience

I smiled that day in hospital as I realized that my waiting as a surgical patient was unexpectedly creating a patient heart within me! In the same way we have to practise being in the presence of God, to discover the very presence of God. It is in waiting we learn to wait. It is quite unlike any other human activity; so often we practise for something through doing more activity, not less. Only in this task of waiting will we learn how to do it, and even then we will resist it, fight it and find it driving us nuts.

One of the most notable differences between people in everyday life and those who have chosen the religious life[6] is the ability of the religious to wait. This is not because their lives are empty: any visitor to a monastery will have realized how busy the life of a religious community can get. Neither is their ability to wait based on the quiet rhythm of prayer, although

I have no doubt at all that it helps. What one perceives is the presence of a patient heart. I have known some who have entered this way of life and I have witnessed them move from impatience to patience, people whose very demeanour has changed as they have learnt through many hours of waiting even more about their vocation to the quieter life. As we begin to develop the gift of waiting, we will either find it too hard and give up altogether, or we will become patient through the waiting and become more naturally those who can wait.

The fruit of the Spirit is love, joy, peace and patience, yet patience is so often a missing element of contemporary church life. Is it, I wonder, because the Church by and large has not learnt how to wait and has not developed, either personally or corporately, the patient heart? In a world of rush, bother and stress, the counter-cultural deeply formed Christian who can bring patience to the bus stop, the trustees' meeting and the sickbed will be incarnating something of the eternal, the slow-time world of the kingdom of God, where eternity flows. It is my express belief that what the Western world needs today more and more is those who can be relied on to move slowly when slowness is required and to provide a deep pool of patience, just as God is patient with his creation.

It is fascinating: right at the pivot point of the Church's embryonic beginnings, when the stirrings of a new chapter are in the air, God wants his children to be still and grow in patience. It is an echo of the pattern of creation that, when everything is set, God rests on the seventh day. Paul urges the Christians in Rome, Corinth, Ephesus and Thessalonica to be patient, to grow in patience. Love, he says, is, before all else, patient (Romans 12.12; 1 Corinthians 13.4; 2 Corinthians 1.6; Ephesians 4.2; 1 Thessalonians 5.14). Patience is much more than an art: it is a beautiful, attractive and transforming way of life. It is so absent from modern life, and yet can impact others in such a way that we should all seek to make it part of who we are.

Waiting develops stillness

As we develop patience, we find a quietude rising within our souls. The Celts speak of 'thin places' where earth and heaven come close. I have found that we can create thin places in our daily life, places that are not so much geographical as supernatural, where earth and heaven come close within us: a contemplative way of coming close to God. This is one of the beauties of learning patience, because becoming still is deeply beneficial to all aspects of our life and sets us up to be more receptive to God and his call.

The psalmist calls out to the frenetic crowd, to the roar of the hastening city, 'Be still, and know that I am God' because even in his day the human heart was impatient and harried. Today that cry is even more needed and relevant than it was then. In 1 Kings 19 Elijah meets God, not in the wind's roar or the earth-shattering earthquake or even in the flames of fire but in the still small voice of eternity. Unless we learn to quieten the heart and to be still within, we shall so often find ourselves missing out on what God has to offer. Had Elijah not patiently waited on the mountain, stilling his anxious heart through the storms, he might not have heard the small whisper of God.

In the twelfth century Bernard of Clairvaux said,

> We should seek to become reservoirs rather than canals. For a canal just allows the water to flow through it, but a reservoir waits until it is filled before overflowing then it can communicate without loss to itself. In the church today, we have many canals but few reservoirs.[7]

Today these words are more prophetic than in his day. Relentless activity, long working hours and overstimulation rob us of the superabundance of God's love, grace, gifts and riches.

From time to time I have been privileged to accompany a Christian friend during the final weeks of his or her life on earth, when faith is all that is left and a quiet inner stillness is evident. This is a 'thin place' where heaven and earth come naturally close – the death and Resurrection of Jesus clearly defining the faith of the dying person. '[God] has also set eternity in the human heart; yet no one can fathom what God has done from beginning to end' (Ecclesiastes 3.11). Perhaps the understanding only becomes simple when the eternal comes close. Maybe we should all spend time reflecting on our finitude in order to understand and allow eternity to rise within us.

It seems as I watch Christian friends and colleagues that 'God makes himself most available to those who make themselves most available to him'.[8] 'Blessed are those who listen to me, watching daily at my doors, waiting at my doorway' (Proverbs 8.34). Making ourselves available to God will involve living confessionally before God *and* waiting upon him often. Jesus says that he is the vine and our task is to abide in him. This is where our eternal awareness meets our willing availability; it is where we learn to surrender and faith is nurtured.

In his book *Waiting on God*,[9] Andrew Murray sums up the essence of 'waiting' as he reflects on his pastoral ministry in South Africa before making a trip saying that he 'had been very impressed by the thought of how, in all our Christianity, personal and public, we need more of God'. He goes on to say what he means by 'more of God', defining it as a 'deeper sense of his presence', a 'more direct contact with him' and ultimately a 'more entire dependence upon him'.

To be still is to somehow come away from the temporal and to dwell in the eternity of God. In 'quiet stillness we stop hearing the murmurings of our own heart, the agendas of our dreams and the distractions of our days'[10] and we become open and alive to God. As Paula Gooder puts it:

> Deep attention to the present cannot help but transform us as we learn – or relearn as the case may be – how to live deeply and truly in the present moment so that we are content to linger in our lives as they are now and not be looking forward, striving onwards to the next goal.[11]

Some years ago a magazine article told of a church leader who saw no new life in his church for the first 11 years. Only then did it begin to flourish, and then it grew. That church became a resource to others around, filling up and sharing from the overflow and superabundance of God's grace. What was God teaching that church leader over those first 11 years? To be patient, to be still, to pray the prayer of relinquishment,[12] to wait on God for his intervention. I suspect that, as a church, they had to learn the holy habit of waiting, while having their faith tried and tested over and over again, while often feeling they were in the wilderness, and yet through it all learning to hold to faith in a God who had not finished with them yet.

Waiting brings forth faithfulness

Waiting on God takes faith; waiting on people takes faith. Before mobile phones were invented we had waited at the station for a friend for 40 minutes. Now the train was just two minutes away from pulling out of King's Cross: only faith made us wait on as the Tannoy announced the doors would be closing, and faith was rewarded as she came running round the corner, breathlessly explaining that her bus had broken down. Faith is tested and faith is tried, and faith, like prayer, has to be intentional, for despite faith being a gift of God, the activity, the life of faith, has to be born of the will. The friend who has texted me as I write this to say that her flat purchase has failed will have to decide whether to give up trusting God or whether to go on faithfully waiting on him, just as Elijah had to decide whether to remain still, patiently waiting for the voice of God, or to give up.

Wait in the city, Jesus says. Will you wait? It invites, even demands, a response. Either Peter will wait or he won't, and the many times that we will be asked this very question by God we will likewise have to decide: will I wait or won't I? In the choosing to wait we choose to live by faith. And in each choice to wait on God we will find subsequent choices simpler. To create waiting as a habit prepares us for who knows what we will have to wait for, but in forming the habit of waiting we will be more readily and more naturally a faithful disciple, a still overflowing reservoir, a patient and more godly follower of Jesus. Not that waiting by itself makes us godly, but this is something I shall explore in the next section, for it is about waiting for a unique God-given gift.

The rush of modern living is giving birth to more and more stress and stress-related illness. In the face of this cultural pressure to live life hard and fast, the godly man or woman will stand out because he or she stands for something else, something 'other' than what is normal. If, through waiting, we become still within and faithful in the way we approach life, we will surely become deeper pools of strength and compassion for those around; we may even become reservoirs. But this will take time, along with watching over our lives and doctrines. The habits explored thus far will lead us into transformation as our hearts first become surrendered to God, then quietly open to his transforming power; heart surgery takes time and spiritual heart surgery takes longer. As these early habits take hold of us, we shall see our hard hearts of stone replaced with hearts of flesh, just as Ezekiel prophesied, and in preparation for the gift that is offered to Peter, you and me.

Waiting for the gift

> He gave them this command: 'Do not leave Jerusalem,
> but wait for the gift my Father promised, which you
> have heard me speak about.'
>
> (Acts 1.4)

As the disciples waited in Jerusalem, they must have been alternately gripped by fear and by faith: fear that the promises would lead nowhere and that Jesus was gone for good, and faith because it was all they had left. The one they had followed had revealed himself to be divine, and to date he had kept his promises and genuinely seemed to love them. He had renewed his promises to them often, regardless of their failings and mistakes.

This is our experience too. Jesus has revealed himself as divine, and the testimony of both the Church and individuals over centuries is that despite our failings and mistakes God continues to love us and his promises stand before us as signs of that love. It is this faithfulness of God that calls out faith within us in our own times of waiting. The disciples, however, are not waiting for the sake of waiting. Jesus in leaving them has told them to stay in the city for the Father's promise to be delivered, and Luke records that Jesus promised God would send the gift of the Holy Spirit upon them. John records how the Spirit is given in response to obedience. The fact that faith eventually wins out over fear in Jerusalem is testament to their spiritual hopes.

If the habit of waiting was just about being still, developing patience and growing in faith, the Church would be full of lovely people but it would lack any real life or power. When Jesus tells Peter and the disciples to wait, it is not in vain; they are to wait in order to be prepared for when the Spirit comes. The days between the Ascension of Jesus and the coming of the Spirit at Pentecost are the most significant in church history, yet it remains a lost season in most churches.

While Lent and Advent have each given rise to many good and godly books, practices, services and traditions that have helped many to grow in holiness, they do not reflect actual biblical times of waiting and preparation. One culminates in the celebration of Jesus' birth and is overwhelmed by secular attention. The other culminates in the Easter Passion and the pivotal story of Jesus' death and Resurrection. I want the Church to give more attention to this short ten-day season of waiting that culminates in the coming of the Holy Spirit. So significant historically is this to the Church and to church history that I believe we are impoverished until our churches take it more seriously. These are without doubt the most important ten days in the life of the Church, for they test the faith of our founders and call forth patience from a group of naturally impatient men, who are amazingly renewed in their waiting. As the Holy

Spirit is given in power and received in humility, there is a divinely appointed collision between the disciples' waiting and the birth of the Church.

Of the fruits of the Holy Spirit, patience is often lacking from many Christians, but it would be true to say that joy is also more absent than it should be. 'For the joy that was set before him he endured the cross, scorning its shame, and sat down at the right hand of the throne of God' (Hebrews 12.2). This same joy is set before us, yet we won't or don't want to endure anything in the journey of life to get it. For Jesus the cross stood between him and eternal joy, but for that joy he endured the cross. It is this very death and Resurrection of Jesus which gives us cause for joy, the deep assurance that all shall be well, that by faith in him we are no longer condemned but set free. Yet this joy eludes us because we are so often not prepared to die to self, to pick up our cross daily and follow Jesus. The life of the flesh, Paul says, is set over against the life of the Spirit. The fruits of the Spirit include peace, patience and joy. Teilhard de Chardin is right in his assertion that 'Joy is the most infallible sign of the presence of God.'

If we really want to live holy lives, if our desire to be Christ-like is authentic, then we have to be equally serious about putting some aspects of our life to death so that the Holy Spirit can be at work in our lives, present in our everyday journey. Too often the Church is more worried about theologically defining itself over against different internal factions than in realizing that each expression brings something to the world-wide body of Christ. We are beginning to see a convergence of teaching on prayer, with enthusiasm for the Bible and a desire to show mercy in the world, and increasingly I see maturity as Christian men and women learn to tease each other about their churchmanship and spiritual heritage. Unless we are Christ-centred, Bible-based people, focused and Spirit-filled, we are not the full expression of Christ's life which he wants us to be. When he declares that he has come that we may have fullness of life (John 10.10) he has no desire to see us cling to our particular safe but impoverished corner of the Church, but to have life in abundance, as he lives life abundantly.

Bernard of Clairvaux uses his image of us being reservoirs, not canals, filled to the brim and overflowing, in a sermon on the Song of Songs where he refers to us being filled with God's overflowing love. Bernard cautions his monks and all Christian pastors not to presume to lead, teach or pastor until they have first mastered the leading and governing of their own lives, and only to teach when they have obtained depth in their own understanding. It is simple wisdom: we need to know God's love in abundance, we need to be filled with the Holy Spirit, we need to 'watch over our doctrine' and open our hearts to whatever the Spirit wants to brings to us, and then open up some more! All that before we might think we have anything to give out.

In Exodus 31.2–3 it is Bezalel who is first recorded as being filled with the Holy Spirit, and this manifests as wisdom, understanding, knowledge and all kinds of skills to make artistic designs for work in gold, silver and bronze. For Bezalel his very life and identity was engendered by the Holy Spirit at work in him. In Deuteronomy 34 the elderly and fading Moses lays hands on Joshua, who in that moment receives the Spirit's wisdom to lead the people after Moses' death. For Joshua the very fulfilment of his vocation depended on receiving the Holy Spirit. Throughout the Old Testament God gives his Holy Spirit to those in leadership or prophetic ministry so that his divine mission may unfold.

In Luke 1 both parents of John the Baptist are filled with the Holy Spirit, Elizabeth when John in her womb first encounters Jesus' presence and Zechariah after months of silently waiting. The New Testament records a change in the way the Holy Spirit is given. Now it is no longer given to just those appointed for special tasks but is poured out on young and old, men and women. It is at Pentecost we see this happen dramatically and we hear Joel's prophetic words recalled: this is God's promise, and it is the promise that brings life to the people of God.

To live an increasingly holy Christian life we need the Spirit to be at work in us too. To know the peace of the cross and the joy of the Resurrection, to be at peace with our own God-given identity so that we overflow towards others, we must exercise the waiting muscle. We must relearn the discipline of waiting obediently for the Spirit's anointing.

This discipline of waiting for the gift is simple. Today many charismatic churches will invite the gathered people to wait on God, to invite the Holy Spirit into their lives; this will often follow a moving and powerful time of sung worship or an inspirational and challenging sermon. However, the Holy Spirit is not dependent on musicians and preachers. I love the Celtic thinking about the Holy Spirit being like a wild goose, untameable and given to its own desires. Surely we are not to rely on the gifts of others for our own occasional personal spiritual top-up. No, it is more simple than that – we are each to practise the discipline of waiting on God, at home and at work, in the morning and the evening, regularly within our own personal pattern of prayer. In this simple way we enter often into the 'divine milieu' where to some extent the Spirit infects us. The disciples waited on God; they found an inner stillness in an upper room, and by their very waiting invited God to send his Spirit upon them. It is that simple for us, whether it is a corner of our flat or a favourite bench in the park. If waiting is in the daily rhythms of life we have taken a key step in opening our lives to God's blessing. This Godward waiting consists of us looking to him as the giver of good gifts and in particular the gift of the Holy Spirit.

The goal of these three holy habits is the transformation of our lives. Contemplative prayer that seeks God's spiritual blessing leads to changed lives. As the Spirit leads us into truth, he will often reveal things about us that are not comfortable to hear. He comes at times as a refiner's fire. While this may be scary it is all the more reason why we are wise to wait on him, so finally let us consider how we might wait upon God for the gift of the Holy Spirit.

Actively waiting

The waiting that God requires is more than simply typified by patience or an inner still faithfulness. Luke records that when John the Baptist appeared the people were waiting expectantly for the Messiah (Luke 3.15); indeed, many Jews are still waiting for him and routinely cry, 'Next year in Jerusalem!' There is not just a belief that he will come but a deeply held expectation. Likewise, the disciples who met with the Messiah and were heeding his command to wait in the city for the Holy Spirit did so in real expectation. Just 16 verses record the manner of their waiting: constant in prayer, watching over their lives and doctrine, they recall God's word and in obedience elect a replacement for Judas. There is a real expectation that the Spirit will come and a very real getting ready for whatever that might mean. This is active waiting. It does not compete with the contemplative manner of waiting, but is born out of it.

Here it is fundamental that we are bigger than the things that divide us. Evangelicals and Charismatics often have little time for contemplation and mystery, while Catholics and Liberals can seem suspicious of the more immediate and outward manifestations of the Holy Spirit. I want to call each of us to the prayer of contemplation, whereby we pray for the sake of prayer, where we set aside the 'work of intercessory prayer' for the joy and privilege of contemplating God in his fullest identity, knowing that as we do so he is looking upon us and our true self. This prayer takes time and is not something to rush into, but neither is it the preserve of the mystics or spiritually mature: it is the most natural form of prayer, if we did but know it. It is the prayer that requires no words and no understanding, just our willingness to 'let go and let God', as the Julian Meetings often say. It is the form of prayer in which our openness to God most allows him to be at work within us; it is the place of transformation.

In letting go of our own agendas and the world's distractions we can actively look to God to come to work within us. This is how our minds will be renewed (Romans 12.1–2). This is where we allow doctrine to shine upon us and to go to work within us; this is how we prepare for the Holy Spirit to fill us. When Jesus preached his Sermon on the Mount and declared that 'Blessed are those who hunger and thirst for righteousness, for they will be filled' (Matthew 5.6) he was telling us that with faith there needs to be a hunger, a desire, an active expectation that Jesus is indeed the bread of life, that he is our righteousness, that only he can fulfil our aching heart's desire and that as we drink from his waters of life we will be satisfied. There has to be that hunger within us, an active expectation. For some this hunger will be birthed in a place of emptiness; for others we have to recognize that our over-satiated lives are not really satisfied at all, and hear the spiritual groans of hunger deep within. This hunger is found so often not in our frustrations or in our desperate searching but in the stillness of the Godward heart. We ought to frequently wait for the Spirit, and as we do this spiritual hunger born out of our *confessional lives* will bubble up within.

Living contemplatively

This second habit of waiting might best be described as living contemplatively. It is not a life of esoteric silence. The ten days for the disciples were after all punctuated with meals, conversation, discussion and laughter. Contemplatives are not always silent, but there is always an inner stillness found in them. A contemplative has found the better way, as Mary does in Luke 10: the way of gazing in patient faithfulness is better than rushing, fussing and striving. *Contemplative living* includes rich times of this waiting prayer. It is the prayer that follows knowledge of God and awareness of self that leads to a self-emptying, a stilling of the heart that we might truly know God in the silence while allowing ourselves to be known by him. It is a readiness to receive words, pictures and the presence and inspiration of the Holy Spirit. It requires attention and time and is rewarded with awe and wonder.

Contemplative living will include many times of simply beholding Jesus and becoming 'lost in wonder, love and praise'. If we can develop this way of living we will have entered the second discipline. This second step on the walk with God is the best and dearest way in which we can come close to God that he may come close to us.

> Contemplation is the way by which we are intimately connected with the pure and perfect love of God which is God's greatest gift to the soul. It is deep and intimate knowledge of God by a union of love – a union in which we learn things about Him that those who have not received the gift of contemplation will never discover until they enter heaven.[13]

4

Walking – the beautiful habit

—————•◦•◦•—————

Then Peter stood up with the Eleven, raised his voice and addressed the crowd: 'Fellow Jews and all of you who live in Jerusalem, let me explain this to you; listen carefully to what I say. These people are not drunk, as you suppose. It's only nine in the morning! No, this is what was spoken by the prophet Joel: "In the last days, God says, I will pour out my Spirit on all people. Your sons and daughters will prophesy, your young men will see visions, your old men will dream dreams."'

(Acts 2.14–17)

One day Peter and John were going up to the temple at the time of prayer – at three in the afternoon. Now a man who was lame from birth was being carried to the temple gate called Beautiful, where he was put every day to beg from those going into the temple courts. When he saw Peter and John about to enter, he asked them for money. Peter looked straight at him, as did John. Then Peter said, 'Look at us!' So the man gave them his attention, expecting to get something from them.

(Acts 3.1–5)

'In the name of Jesus, walk'

I have no greater joy than to hear that my children
are walking in the truth.

(3 John 4)

On 11 February 1990 the world watched Nelson Mandela make the long lonely walk towards and then through the prison gates of Victor Verster prison. Finally, aged 71, his long walk to free-

54

dom was becoming a reality. It would be fulfilled in two stages, however. On that day as he walked through the prison gates to be greeted by the crowds, his own freedom was secure, bringing to an end 27 years in prison. In his heart, however, lay a deep vocation to work ceaselessly for the freedom of black South Africans, the end of apartheid. Only when that was achieved would his long walk be complete.

So we come to the last of these three habits for the Christian disciple: the habit of walking. It is one that each of us grows into at our own pace, but only if we set our hearts upon doing so. It is perhaps a way of life as much as it is a life-forming habit. It is the habit of 'living in the promise of freedom' which Jesus desires for all who become his followers. In order to enter it we need to reflect on a walk that Jesus made, the walk of one man which more than any other changed the politics of the world: the walk from the courtrooms of Pilate to the hill of Calvary. Like Mandela's walk 2,000 years later, Jesus' walk was rooted in a deep sense of vocation. But Jesus' walk of freedom was not just about releasing one colour in one country: it was to liberate men and women, boys and girls, the world over. Peter witnessed this walk first hand. He saw what came next, the suffering and ignominy of the cross, and he was to discover that on the other side lay a new life for Christ and a freedom for many as a result of this one man's lonely walk and triumphant Resurrection.

Peter's own story this time begins indoors with the other followers of Jesus. Acts tells us that they are together for the ten days, their hearts patiently waiting, faithfully leaning into God and his promise, expectantly 'holding on' for the gift, surrendering their careers, livelihoods and dignity for the one in whom they have chosen to put their trust. And then they are rewarded – the flames of fire touch them and a sound like the rushing of a wind announces the coming of the Holy Spirit upon Jesus' disciples.

The more I read this account, the more I am reminded of the moment when the Ark of the Covenant is placed in the

Temple in 1 Kings 8, with the priests there unable to perform their unique and privileged duty as the cloud fills the place and engulfs them. In Acts we are told of flames and wind, only this time the inhabitants of the holy meeting place are enabled to perform new things in the power of the Spirit: each will speak in strange tongues, with a language unique to each given so that the gospel may be understood by the international crowd of visitors gathered in Jerusalem for the feast. This time it is not a debilitating event for a partisan few but an empowering occasion for the benefit of the whole world – and what happens next? Luke tells us that following the charismatic commotion caused by the disciples' deep sense of joy and the vocal manifestation of the Spirit in each of them, Peter stands up to speak.

Our final habit in Peter's transformation is discernible when he stands up with the Eleven and raises his voice to address the crowd. The first time of speaking publicly often has a mingling sense of both excitement and fear about it, with the speaker wondering if people will listen, hoping preparations are enough, hair tingling with anticipation. For Peter there have been ten days of remembering the stories and all that Jesus taught them, but now there seems no time at all, barely minutes with which to prepare – the moment has arrived suddenly, the waiting is over. While it is the Pentecost feast of first fruits, the day of harvest thanksgiving, it has all been very much more sudden and dramatic than he ever imagined, and now the crowds are jeering and calling for an explanation. Peter stands and raises his voice, and in that moment acknowledges before hundreds that he is a follower of Jesus. He also lets it be known that he is foolishly trusting Jesus, just as Noah long before stood out for his solo act of foolishly trusting God; he is not ashamed for the world to know. He stands to address the crowd, and as he opens his mouth to speak he is given a confidence and a message to declare: a new age has dawned, the last days are here, the promise of Isaiah, Ezekiel and Joel has arrived, God's Spirit is being poured liberally on all people for the first time in history, and now it is evident that 'everyone who calls on the name of the Lord will be saved' (Acts 2.21).

Standing to address the crowd is Peter's first step to walking with God – if you want to walk you have to stand first! For Peter it is a declaration of intent: he is planning to walk forward and address the crowd. Rather more significantly, he is choosing to choose, and he is choosing to choose God. This publicly intentional lifestyle that he is stepping into will reach a fuller expression in Acts 3: the first recorded miracle of the Church, the moment when new wine is poured into old wine skins. Peter and John are observing the old pattern of going to pray at the time and place of prayer, when they encounter a man, lame from birth, physically unable to walk. Peter is unlike the priest and the Levite who pass by on the other side of the road: he is the Good Samaritan, Spirit-filled, with nothing to offer but his faith. They look at each other and Peter says, 'Silver or gold I do not have, but what I do have I give you. In the name of Jesus Christ of Nazareth, walk,' and with that Peter inhabits the life he was born to live. Peter's life is transformed from doubting, clumsy fisherman to confident, faithful, Spirit-filled ambassador, irrefutable proof that God by sending his Spirit can do amazing things with un-amazing people. From now on Peter will be known by the fruit of his life; it is the same transformation that is on offer to each of us and to which all of us are called by Jesus. And it starts for us as it did for the crippled man, when we stand to walk. For make no mistake, two lives were transformed in this miracle: Peter inhabited his God-given identity and a man crippled from birth walked and jumped and praised God.

Peter had succumbed to the buffeting waves and wind last time he had sought to walk in faith, but this time he is walking in surrender to God, his eyes open to the world of need around him, its turbulence no longer the cause of his sinking but rather the call to his heart which releases a Spirit-filled love. Jesus had told them once before that by their fruit his true followers would be known. The first recorded miracle of the

Church is the fruit of a man who has opened his heart to God, and his hard, brittle, fragile heart is replaced by one of flesh, a strong beating muscle of grace. He is a new creation and is learning each day to walk as Noah, Enoch and many others before him have done. Peter's faith and example would lead countless more in the future to join him. What he had begun that day on his way to the Temple at three in the afternoon would be told around the planet. Peter was finally 'walking with God' and he was drawing others to walk with him too.

When Peter looks at the man crippled from birth lying by the Beautiful gate, he sees the potential that God sees in us all. Born unable to walk, the unnamed man looks attentively to Peter, expecting some money to survive the day. He gets so much more: he receives an abundance of life. Peter gives a simple command to him and to all the unnamed who have yet to walk with God: 'In the name of Jesus Christ of Nazareth, walk' (Acts 3.6). That command, invitation and gift has been spoken by Peter across the nations and the generations to us all; no wonder it happens at the gate called Beautiful.

Why is walking important?

> And what does the LORD require of you? To act justly
> and to love mercy and to walk humbly with your God.
> (Micah 6.8)

I love walking. I am drafting this the day before I head off to the Lake District for a three-day walking retreat among the mountains of Red Pike, Skiddaw, Scafell and many others whose solid enormity evokes in me something of the awesome and unchanging nature and power of God. I will pull on my walking boots and grab my day bag and head up away from the lakes, past the sheep folds, over stiles and through streams, passing small tarns and on towards the glorious and windy mountain peaks. So often on these annual trips we find ourselves walking through damp mist and worse; at times we stand on the mountain top as the view disappears in the clouds. Yet the following year we set off again through sun, rain or snow, because reaching the top is only part of the joy – it is the climb, the walks, the being outdoors, the mini journeys over hills and rivers that we go for. While getting to the top is a treat, the day is not spoilt if we don't, because quite simply we go mountain walking in order to go walking.

Walking with God is found throughout the Bible, sometimes in reality, as when God walks in the garden with Adam and Eve, and at other times metaphorically, as when it describes the way in which the kings of Israel either did or didn't walk with God all their days. When Paul says to the Galatians, 'But I say, walk by the Spirit, and do not gratify the desires of the flesh' (5.16, RSV) he knows it will require them to 'watch and pray, for the spirit is willing but the flesh is weak'. If we are honest this is our struggle; our spirits are willing and ready to follow Jesus but the temptations and distractions of this life get in the way, and we are weak to the point of failure. We need to watch our lives and doctrine and wait on God for the infilling of his Holy Spirit to forgive, transform and empower us, and having waited we are ready to walk by the Spirit.

It was February 2006 when I travelled to Bangladesh to understand something of the country from which so many of my neighbours had originated or which they at least looked back to as their homeland. We arrived in Dhaka for my first real encounter with that part of the world. The overnight stop in Kolkata had barely prepared me for travelling along the overcrowded roads and pavements, with people everywhere. In five weeks of travelling to cities, towns and remote parts of the countryside I barely ever had a view that didn't include people walking, talking, cycling, carrying and working the fields. For part of our time we stayed as guests at the Baptist school for blind girls in Mirpur, a busy, dusty district of Dhaka.

The hospital was built in a quadrangle with a square of grass in the middle and a broken concrete path running round the square of grass. It was only a few months after the Danish newspaper *Jyllands-Posten* had published cartoons that had offended many Islamic groups. Dhaka's frequent protests can sound quite threatening to a white guy with blond hair exploring alone on foot! Back in my room drinking mango lassi after witnessing the latest noisy protest, I looked out of the window to see Manju, the director of this amazing school, walking round the square path. She was accompanied by her husband and the assistant director; round and round they went. Night after night they did this: half an hour of walking, sometimes talking, sometimes in silence. On my last evening I joined them and the memory is for ever etched in my mind.

Why did they do it? Why did three people in their fifties walk for half an hour each evening around a dry patch of grass in the midst of a teeming city at the end of a day of caring for and teaching some of the most vulnerable people in Bangladesh? Because it was good for them, was the reply they gave. It was left to me to work out what they meant. It was certainly a moderate form of physical exercise; it cleared the head; the conversation was often a daily reflection; it was also a gift of time that they gave to each other regardless of other duties and temptations. But above all it was about just being together, walking and spending time in the presence of those with whom they wanted to share their life's journey.

Walking with God is important for exactly these reasons. It is healthy, for it is what we were made for and to live any other way will bring us stress and dis-ease. It is the way in which, with God, we can clear our heads, turning over with him the thoughts, ideas, struggles, hopes and people of our day. It is a gift of time that we can give to God, the daily acknowledgement that among the many things we have to do and attend to the most important is to take time to be with our heavenly Father: there is quite simply no one more important that we will meet today, there is no one more powerful that we can talk with and there is no one who loves us more than he, so not to walk with him each day begins to seem a little absurd. But perhaps above all else walking with God is about being in his presence and consciously deciding to travel through life with him.

When Peter stood up on the day of Pentecost he was readying himself to walk with God. The crowds that he spoke to were not the most important focus for him that day; the speech he gave them, while recorded for ever as the first sermon of the Church, was not for him the great achievement of the morning. Peter was living out what he had failed to do months earlier: this was the fulfilment of the prophetic act of walking on the water, and the redemption of the courtyard scene. Today he had Jesus in his focus, today his faith was intact and he wouldn't sink below the waves or challenges of life as he set out on the long walk of freedom. The standing up before the crowd and the sermon were primarily an offering to God. In the words of Frances Young, 'If we do not go forward we go backward.' Peter was going forward; he was offering his life to God. We all have to choose our journey – there is no standing still. Moses reminds Israel:

> I set before you today life and prosperity, death and destruction. For I command you today to love the LORD your God, to walk in obedience to him, and to keep his commands . . . Now choose life, so that you and your children may live and that you may love the LORD your God, listen to his voice, and hold fast to him.
> (Deuteronomy 30.15–16, 19–20)

Let us not go down in history like Jehoram and Ahaziah, who both walked in the ways of their ancestors and did evil in the sight of the Lord (2 Kings 8) rather than choosing to walk in the ways of God, as Azariah did (2 Kings 15). To take the language of 2 Kings, let us be remembered for doing what is right in the eyes of the Lord so that in death we might rest with our fathers.

Walking

> Yes, LORD, walking in the way of your laws, we wait for you; your name and renown are the desire of our hearts.
> (Isaiah 26.8)

So our last habit, the discipline of walking with God, is the purpose for which the Spirit comes upon us. It is authentic Christian life. But unless we first watch ourselves and our doctrine, unless we turn to God in prayer waiting with open hearts for his transforming Spirit, we will not walk far with God at all.

There is a strong sense in British society today that we can 'do it' alone. Nike etched the phrase into our hearts, while the Thatcher and Blair years moulded the economic landscape around this ideology. I meet many people in the heart of London who believe they can live purely out of their own strength. They are too guarded to seek help from others and have all but given up believing that anyone else would want to help them altruistically. This pervasive (or perverse) sense of self-reliance leaves more people lonely today than ever before; it leads many to emotional and physical breakdown; it lies behind the increase in stress and stress-related illness. And yet bizarrely these same people are often addicted to alcohol, TV, work, shopping and wealth-chasing. The sense of breakdown in our community and social order spilt on to the streets during the summer of 2011 – part of a global turning point as economies go bust and the old 'survival of the fittest' mentality adds to the crisis and we discover that much of humanity is both unwilling and unable to cope with the burgeoning needs of a growing and ageing global population. Prayer is not the only thing we can do in the face of this tragic meltdown, but it is the right place to start. Prayer is an acknowledgement that we cannot do life alone. It is the activity of those who believe that with God we are better able to live our lives and contribute to society than if we try to do so in our own strength alone.

Walking with God is the biblical image of a life that is prayerful, and a prayerful life is quite simply a life that is 'full of prayer', one that is frequently 'leaning into God' – a life lived by someone who is not trying to do it alone but who believes in community and believes that community starts with the Trinity. Essentially it is the old proverb, 'Though one may be overpowered, two can defend themselves. A cord of three strands is not quickly broken' (Ecclesiastes 4.12). A life lived in close proximity to God will be a life of humility and generosity; it will be a life that has to become undefended because we are known intimately by him and cannot hide ourselves from his love. What's more, we have an advocate in Christ who represents us to God the Father and has already taken our broken humanity into the heavenly realms.

We will become so much more ready to face the challenges and strangers of tomorrow. As Paul says to the fledgling Roman church, 'we are more than conquerors through him who loved us' (Romans 8.37). This life not only has a security of its own but is a blessing to those around. The marriage service talks of marriage as a way of life that 'enriches society and strengthens community'. I would contend that an authentic relationship with God does the same: it's the way he would like us to live and to have the greatest impact on the world around us. It is why some parts of the Church remember the lives of saints and martyrs: they lived lives that 'enriched society and strengthened community'. A modern-day saint I was privileged to know was Lily; she immersed herself in prayer each morning and spent the rest of the day walking with God, even in her eighties helping at the church kids' club tuck shop, and encouraging her ageing peers in the day centre to look to him who offers lasting hope.

The Bible uses the term 'walking with God' over 200 times – more in earlier translations, as later ones seem increasingly to substitute 'live' for 'walk'. For instance, when Watchman Nee wrote *Sit, Walk, Stand* he didn't have the New International Version of the Bible. Thank goodness, for the section of his book that encourages us to walk is drawn from eight references to the word in Ephesians. Today the word 'live' has been substituted for almost all of them in modern translations. The call to 'walk with God' is no accident; throughout Scripture the metaphor takes us to a deeper understanding of life with God. It begins when Adam and Eve are cast out of the Garden of Eden and become wanderers, a nomadic people who will wander the earth and who prefigure all our restless wanderings. We are told that Noah was a righteous man of faith who walked with God and by so doing he was spared, that humanity might flourish again one day. Abraham's journey, beginning in Haran, is the continuing journey of a nomadic people who sometimes choose to walk with God in response to his promise. Moses, too, walks with God, leading Israel from slavery in Egypt into a 40-year wandering with God to the Promised Land.

You may feel these stories are dated, coming as they do before the invention of trains and planes, but I make no apology. Today, as well as coping with the rampant individualized approach to life, many are also struggling to keep up with a pace of life that is too full and fast. Slowing down to walk may just slow us down in other ways too.

St Paul of the Cross founded the Passionists, a Roman Catholic missionary community. One of their houses is in Jamaica and it is here that Fr Richard Leary served for 20 years. He was surprised on arriving to discover that the community's rule prescribed two half-hour solitary walk periods each day in order to relieve both mind and body. He himself kept the rule for the duration of his time in that community, and quietly walking with God became a key part of his discipleship – indeed, in time it became also a time of witness, just as St Paul of the Cross had hoped. Inspired by Micah 6.8 he had sought to gather his community together under the cross and teach them how to walk with God. It is no surprise, then, that a common Jamaican phrase on parting from a friend is 'Walk well'.

Physically choosing to walk each day with God for half an hour is a great pattern and full of opportunity. It will transform our lives, but it is not the whole picture, for even those times need depth and shape if they are going to be richly beneficial to us. What exactly does it mean to walk with God? Those in Scripture who walk with God are seeking to live continually in his presence, living out a relationship with him that is stronger and richer if characterized by the metaphor of walking. Our relationship with God is always at its best when we are 'in step with him'.

Walking with God is 'walking'

Walking as a metaphor for living brings some obvious connotations which, when used to measure our spiritual journey, lead on to some immediate applications. For most of us walking is simple and comes early in our lives, usually about the age of one, but talking – the ability we use in our prayer lives more than anything else – does not come until nearly a year later. Perhaps this order has something to teach us. The attributes of walking that I believe we might usefully apply to our spiritual lives are that it involves travel and is not static; it is rhythmic; it has a pattern and as such is habitual; and, last, it is physical and involves little of our head but all of our body. Perhaps if our spiritual lives are about travelling, if we develop a natural rhythm and if we involve our whole bodies rather than just our heads, our whole life will become richer and more engaged with God.

While many are shaped by a continuing conscious journey with God, learning new things about him, being led by him to places and people that are part of his plan for us, many others have a spiritual life which is more like a stagnant pool to which they reluctantly return to sip from stale waters.

Too many quiet days are spent rewriting spiritual rules or seeking to impose impossible new patterns of prayer, believing that somehow they will take us closer to God, when in fact walking needs to find its own pattern. The shape of our spirituality needs attention, yes, but often once we attend to it honestly we discover it needs just a simple tweaking, some simple changes to the person we are naturally made by God to be. He has set eternity within us and we need to understand it in order to enjoy it.

As a hiker there is no point me trying to walk at a speed I am not built for or to stretch my legs over rocks that are clearly bigger than my stride, yet this is what countless folk do all the time with their prayer lives. We seek to grab a pattern off the shelf and apply it to ourselves, squeezing into scaffolding that doesn't fit. When Forrest Gump begins to run, the leg callipers he has worn for years are no longer needed: they no longer suit the natural development of his legs. If you have sought to establish a pattern of prayer and struggled, it may just be that you need to look again at the natural rhythms of your daily life, the seasons in which you live, and adjust accordingly to find a pattern that is really you. A friend of mine used to pray at midnight: no interruptions and not too many distractions, but actually what mattered most was that it suited him.

To see prayer as a physical activity is also very important. Too often, for too many, prayer is about finding a moment of stillness in a comfy chair or on an uncomfortable prayer stool when internally we are anything but still. We might seek God in a retreat house miles from home, perfectly focused with a candle and an icon, in a comfortable set of clothes, yet as we settle down to pray it escapes us, lasting no more than a few moments before it is snatched away by distraction. Exhaustion and distraction all too often are the unseen enemies of our faith, the fiery darts of the evil one. We are whole beings and God wants us to come to him whole, body, mind and soul. Too often we try to come to him with our head alone, turning prayer into a cognitive activity, and wonder why it doesn't work. Kneeling, standing, moving, singing, dancing, lying down, walking – all can help us focus on God far more than sitting among distractions or falling asleep, as in Gethsemane.

The act of walking, with its rhythmic habitual pattern, can be a physical echo of our heartbeat; it can mirror the movement of the waves on the seashore; it will improve our breathing and often it follows its pattern. I have had some of my sweetest encounters with God when walking.

Our spiritual life also needs to be in motion: it needs rhythm, pattern and habit; it needs to be a physical as well as a mental and emotional engagement with God. I recall being on retreat and a monk telling me that the daily pattern of prayers had been a struggle for the first few years until he realized they would always be there and always like that, and he began to walk to the chapel at the sound of the bell, readying himself rather than rushing to be there on time with resentment in his heart. He told me that now when prayers are over in the chapel they are rarely over in his heart, with the rhythm of the monastic day no longer a series of interruptions but rather focal points that mark out the shape of a *life of prayer* – no longer simply a *pattern of prayer* but refreshing water stops along the way. I admire his prayerful life. There is a picture of prayer which describes the words of our prayers as the banks of a river, leading us towards God, the words slowly becoming further apart until they are not needed as the river enters the sea. Perhaps the patterns we adopt to hold our prayers will one day lead to an overflowing prayerfulness that reshapes those very patterns.

Brother Lawrence says,

> I make it my priority to persevere in His holy presence, wherein I maintain a simple attention and a fond regard for God, which I may call an actual presence of God. Or to put it another way, it is an habitual, silent, and private conversation of the soul with God. This gives me much joy and contentment.[14]

Brother Lawrence had been a soldier before becoming a religious, partly crippled during his military career and then ironically working as a footman! God takes our weaknesses and turns them into his opportunities, if we let him and if we make that all-important decision to commit our way to becoming his way and to strive to walk alongside him. Brother Lawrence persevered in his physical movement, and as he did so he also persevered with his holy habits. In Galatians Paul tells us to 'keep in step' with the Spirit, inviting us to this particular healthy rhythmic pattern of life.

Walking with God is 'with God'

How far is God from us?
We are only ever a moment away from God.[15]

One thing is profoundly true of the habit of 'walking with God': it involves us in being 'with him'. It requires a commitment to be in his presence, seeking his company and living in the light of his countenance. It is worth remembering just how keen he is to walk with us. When Adam and Eve are hiding in the garden, ashamed of their mistakes, God chooses to walk there; his preparedness to walk alongside us is not in any way diminished by our sinfulness, weakness, history or failing. Psalm 56 reminds us: 'For you have delivered me from death and my feet from stumbling, that I may walk before God in the light of life' (v. 13). God's greatest desire is that we may live as Enoch lived. This is a way of understanding the 'fullness of life' that Jesus came to give us. When we walk this earth with God it is the clearest evidence that Christ's resurrection power is at work within us, that eternity is ours now, that the divine presence is our animation, preparing us to walk right into heaven unhindered. It is for this that God delivers us from the entanglement of sin.

When we choose to walk with a friend it often means crossing the road to join that friend, or waiting on the corner for him or her to catch us up, or hurrying along the pavement to catch someone up ourselves. It involves adjusting our journey and having consideration for our friend, acknowledging that we are no longer alone and that being 'with' someone else is better, most often for both of us. This metaphor for living is valuable as God invites us to walk with him. He knows that in order to do so we will have to realize both his presence and his omnipresence, we will have to cross the road, we will have to wait for him and sometimes hurry to catch him up. Above all else, we will have to adjust our stride to keep in step with him: we will have to consider him, exercising 'other awareness'. This is the way of life that Brother Lawrence found and then encouraged others to find.

God is serious about having a relationship with each and every one of us. He longs for a continual conversation with us about even the smallest of things. He has crossed the road and come close to us in human form. He has waited patiently for us to catch up with his hopes and dreams for us and he wants us to walk the rest of our days with him. The question that this discipline asks more than any other is, 'Are we serious about having a relationship with Jesus?'

Too many people give up on the journey of faith because they haven't truly asked themselves this question. Church is great for many, certain Christian friends are a real blessing, corporate worship can lift the soul; but at the end of the day the Christian faith is about friendship with Jesus. It is out of a strong bond with God that some of us are equipped and enabled to face the complexities and struggles of life on earth. It is out of an unending walk with God, a continuing life in his presence, a continual conversation with God that we are fashioned fit for heaven. Brother Lawrence says,

> There is not in the world a kind of life more sweet and delightful than that of a continual conversation with God. Only those can comprehend it who practice and experience it. Yet I do not advise you to do it from that motive. It is not pleasure which we ought to seek in this exercise. Let us do it from a principle of love, and because it is God's will for us.[16]

Clement of Alexandria said, 'Prayer is keeping company with God'; today he might rephrase it as 'Try hanging out with God.' It works. Paul's exhortation to 'keep in step with the Spirit' is a *hanging out* in that place, and one whereby our own lives become richer and more infused with the power of God; it is where the fruit of the Spirit grows best. The psalmist says, 'Seven times a day I look to you', Daniel settled by the window facing Jerusalem three times a day to pray, and Paul tells the Thessalonians to 'pray continually'. The two shortest verses in the Bible are 'Jesus wept' in John 11.35 and 'Pray continually' in 1 Thessalonians 5.17, one reminding us of Jesus' passion for us, the other encouraging us to respond in love for Jesus.

Walking with God is communal

Much of the way we live today is divided between the private and public realms. Our politicians and celebrities crave publicity while at the same time demanding their privacy, but it is not that simple and it was never meant to be. As followers of Jesus, we more than most should have an integrated view of life. In Jesus the divine and human come together, the personal and corporate meet, for he is at once the unique person of Jesus Christ while at the same time one of the three persons of the Trinity. The public and private meet, too, constantly informing each other, with the private personal prayer leading into public ministry that drives him back to prayer. These life-defining characteristics of need inform our understanding of humanity. Our broken humanity is redeemed in Jesus and redefined by his cross and Resurrection: the temporal and eternal, human and divine, personal and corporate, private and public are for ever joined. We each have a personal life to live, but to think we can separate it from others and live without reference to the communities we are called to and a part of will simply lead to greater degrees of loneliness and stress as we try to live at odds with our very own humanity.

Walking with God is communal. While walking with God is something I might personally choose to do, so it is for millions of others. He is passionate towards each and every one of us, almost greedy, wanting millions more to make the same choice. When Peter chose to summon up his courage and preach that first sermon, he was choosing to stand up among a cloud of witnesses. There are three aspects to this communal aspect of walking with God: it is communal in the present, across time and by invitation.

The first is obvious: there are at any one time millions of people seeking to walk with God. Facebook, the social networking site, was excited in the autumn of 2011 to boast that it had half a billion hits on one day, and yet for years God has rarely known a day with fewer than half a billion people praying to him. Knowing that we are among many who are setting out each morning to live the day in the presence of God will bring us comfort and keep us humble. We are not like some polar explorer going it alone but much more like a group of cyclists linked by mobile phone, each setting out on slightly different routes to the same ultimate destination. In knowing this, comfort comes from the assurance that we are not alone even when apart. In quite the opposite way to that of an Arctic explorer who may be tempted to return proud at having gone alone where many cannot go, we are likely to be humble in the certain knowledge that we are treading a well-worn path towards a very well-populated throne room. Walking with God aware of this communal aspect can transform us into being comfortably reassured and also humble alongside those we meet each day. This is surely one of the ways in which the fruit of the Spirit will be brought forth in our lives. For Anglicans there is a memory of the days of the Book of Common Prayer, when around the world on waking believers would use the same prayers in chapels, churches, front rooms and train carriages, knowing that their prayers were both personal and corporate, taking part in a dislocated but nonetheless profoundly shared daily experience of God.

Rather harder to grasp than the communal present is the 'communal across time'. The writer to the Hebrews draws a helpful picture by reciting the lives and acts of the great champions of faith and then summarizing: 'since we are surrounded by such a great cloud of witnesses, let us throw off everything that hinders and . . . run . . . the race' (12.1). It is in this sense that the Church is never static in one generation. In a very simple sense the character and writings of the New Testament have been found among us throughout our history: Elizabeth Fry left a legacy of prison reform; Lord Shaftesbury his Christian philanthropy; and more recently John Stott his thoughtful approach to theology and mission. So our walk with God, who is both within and beyond time, means that, though it may seem mysterious, we are in the company of those who have gone before and walked with God. I believe that in God we can know this company of saints, just as at the Communion table we are partaking in a never-ending meal, a foretaste of the heavenly banquet at which time and space will no longer separate us. Knowing this will make our walk with God more confident, hopeful, bold and faithful. We stand with martyrs, we hang out among spiritual giants and we walk with holy heroes. Our hope is in the Lord alone but our company is with countless others who have trusted him; the eschatological family is huge, the heavenly picnic vast at which one day we will finally sit down after our walking.

Third, then, our walk with God is 'communal by invitation'. We are only ever walking with God because he has invited us to do so. His voice, his call, his invitation was for many of us heard through the words of a friend or family member. Someone somewhere said to us, through words, actions or both, 'Come and walk with God, as I am trying to do.' Our decision to walk with him will often reflect an example set before us, or be shaped by a particular Christian who inspired us. It was like that when Peter and John found themselves at the gate called Beautiful. Their walk and their words inspired a man crippled from birth, one who had never walked, who sensed in the openness of their lives an invitation to join them. He stopped them and they put into words the invitation he had unknowingly longed for: 'What I do have I give you. In the name of Jesus Christ of Nazareth, walk.'

Peter has learnt not only to walk with God but to do so communally. What he has found is not for him alone: his prayer life is not about his individual piety but, as it always is, about the kingdom of God breaking into and through his life. Jesus said that it was by our fruits that we shall be known. Acts 3 depicts fruitful Christian living: it is walking honestly and openly with God, it is communal and it is invitational. Each of us is invited to become an inviter. Our transformative habits will not just form us into reassured, humble and confident believers but they will also lead us into fruitful lives that will add to the numbers of those who walk with God. This unnamed lame man at the gate responds to the miracle of healing by praising God; in so doing he reveals that through his years of begging he has become aware of who he is and who God is, and in the moment that he is transformed he cannot but reach out to God, for he knows God alone has changed his life.

Brother Lawrence, St Paul of the Cross and many of our heroes have sought to walk simply with God, not because the Bible tells them to but because by so doing they please him, and love him with their whole lives, and by making this choice they love his world too. This desire for God and for his world will be found at the heart of any who truly walk with him, and it brings him pleasure.

> I walk before God simply, in faith, with humility
> and with love; and I apply myself diligently to do
> nothing and think nothing which may displease Him.
> (Brother Lawrence)

5

Holy habits in daily life

Whoever wants to be my disciple must deny themselves
and take up their cross daily and follow me.

(Jesus – Luke 9.23)

There is no messing about with Jesus. There is fun, laughter
and joy to be had with him but sometimes he is very serious.
If we want to follow him it will involve a daily decision. I
wonder if the disciples had any real idea what he was talking
about. You must deny yourself, take up your cross daily, and
if you want to save your life you must first lose it. This must
have only begun to make sense during those ten days when
they waited for the Holy Spirit. Daily resisting the temptation
to give up and return to their former ways of living, each day
choosing to wait for the Spirit, the disciples were losing more
and more of their old life and allowing more and more the
power of the Resurrection to be at work within them.

For us too there is a daily need to pick up our cross, let go
of ourselves and let God into our lives. When I am struggling
to write a sermon, I find I just need to down tools, close the
books, sit with the passage of Scripture and wait on God – it
works. If only we could each find ways to sit with God before
the day gets under way, before the project gets a grip on us,
before the world clouds our very vision. The Christian life is
so much about intention: 90 per cent of prayer is choosing to
set time aside for Jesus. This is the hardest decision in setting
out on the road of Christian spirituality and yet it has the most
far-reaching impact.

Someone has calculated that we make on average 5,000 decisions a day, many of them subconscious, lots of them habitual. Having considered three holy habits to make a part of our day we must each find how best to pattern our day and our prayers, for this is essential if we are serious about daily taking up our cross. Let us remember that Jesus is full of grace and compassion; if we fail to turn to him he doesn't instantly consign us to the realm of the dead but waits for us, as he did for Peter on the beach. Jesus is serious: if we want to follow him he asks us to turn to him each day, saying that unless we do we will by default allow our lives to be shaped by temporal qualities that will quickly form a worldly and wrong attitude that we can do life without him, that by gaining our own lives we are saving our own lives, for 'what good is it for someone to gain the whole world, yet forfeit their soul?' (Mark 8.36). Paul reminds us that our minds and lives are to be fashioned by heaven, not earth:

> Since, then, you have been raised with Christ, set your hearts on things above, where Christ is, seated at the right hand of God. Set your minds on things above, not on earthly things. For you died, and your life is now hidden with Christ in God.
>
> (Colossians 3.1–3)

The disciples who first heard Jesus' daily challenge were of course Jewish. For them prayer was already a daily habit; even away from the synagogue there were set morning and evening prayers to be said by all observant Jews. The day would begin, 'Blessed art thou, O Lord our God, King of the universe, who hast hallowed us by thy commandments', a prayer watching God and proclaiming his nature, but also declaring that his commandments will shape our world. Likewise the evening prayer begins, 'Master of the Universe, behold I forgive everyone who has injured me, and may no one be punished because of his wrong to me': this time a prayer watching over our life and living confessionally.

This is living by grace and it cracks open the human heart when it is found. This was the way Jesus prayed each evening, closing his daily prayers:

> I place my soul within his palm,
> before I sleep as when I wake,
> and though my body I forsake,
> I rest in the Lord in fearless calm.[17]

Some years ago, when travelling in Bangladesh, I found myself one night reluctantly lying down to sleep in a stranger's rather forbidding and unsettling house in the Bangladeshi countryside, miles from anywhere and with no means of travel or communication. Our driver had abandoned us and the owner of the house had disappeared – I wasn't even sure it was his. That night I wrote a prayer I still use, but had I had an already established pattern such as these Jewish night prayers I would not have needed to, for not only are they Godward in thought but they instil peace through their own crafting. The problem today is that many of our prayers lack the habit required for the Scriptures and prayers to embed themselves in our hearts, that they might welcome us and bring us peace.

Today committed Jews still pray morning and evening, punctuating the day so that they are never more than a few hours from a time of prayer. The Jewish faith being as much at home in the home as in the synagogue, the daily routines and household activities of everyday life are never far from the time or the place of prayer. For us, having a pattern like this that turns to Jesus throughout the day wherever we are holds and brings the believer regularly into a God space.

Today many Christians already have a God space in their daily routine. If you are among them then consider shaping those routines around the three patterns of transformative prayer explored here. If you haven't found routines that work for you then consider a few days in a monastic setting alongside those who certainly have. 'Seven times a day I praise you,' the psalmist declares in Psalm 119.164, and this is the pattern of many religious houses. If a few days away is too much then maybe you can take a few hours away from routine: a quiet morning in a coffee shop might be just the space you need to reflect on the patterns of life and prayer that you could sink into more fully and frequently with a little tweaking.

Once we have a daily routine in sight it is good to consider morning and evening prayers (known as a daily office in established churches). One of my heroes is Daniel, who prayed three times a day. While captive and exiled in Babylon, Daniel sought to maintain his first love for God even when King Darius decreed laws that aimed to squash it. We are told that Daniel went home to his upstairs room where the windows opened towards Jerusalem. Three times a day he got down on his knees and prayed, giving thanks to his God, just as he had always done (Daniel 6.10). Pausing three times a day to step into the presence of the Living God would be to create a delightfully refreshing habit.

Jesus' desire is to meet with us daily; to have our company morning, noon and night would please him even more. When Jesus teaches his friends to pray he encourages them to say, 'Give us today our daily bread' (Matthew 6.11); a prayer that is only effective for a day will need to be said every day! His assumption was obvious. The Jewish day starts at nightfall and we might begin there too, with our first habit. As we watch over the day that is ending we are watching over our life, as Paul urged Timothy. We reflect, confess and offer it to God, asking forgiveness for ourselves and covenanting with him to forgive those who have offended us. A simple form of the examen that I use is to ask three questions that emerge out of Colossians 3:

1 Does the peace of Christ rule in my heart?
2 Does the word of Christ dwell in me richly?
3 Does all I do bear the name of Christ?

These simple questions allow me to make amends before God, shake the day from my mind, hand it over to him and lie down to sleep resting in his changelessness.

Rising in the morning we would do well to stand in God's presence and set the day before him, echoing the morning synagogue prayer and acknowledging that it is his world and it is his words that will shape us best to live in it. The morning is the time for most of us to watch over our doctrine, and having freshly considered God's person and purposes we wait with open hearts for the inpouring of his Holy Spirit equipping us for the day ahead. Pausing in contemplation of God's grace is honouring to God and renewing for us.

> Whatever is true, whatever is noble, whatever is right, whatever is pure, whatever is lovely, whatever is admirable – if anything is excellent or praiseworthy – think about such things. Whatever you have learned or received or heard from me, or seen in me – put it into practice. And the God of peace will be with you.
>
> (Philippians 4.8–9)

Surely the best way we are made ready for the day that lies ahead is to be lost for a while in knowing and remembering the love of God, then resting in that same love, leaning into the wind of the Spirit. Only then are we divinely prepared for the day ahead.

We would each do well to take time in the middle of the day to check that we are walking in step with the Spirit (Galatians 5.16, 25). The days I finish most tired, stressed, depressed and lonely are the ones where I have wandered out of communion with my heavenly Father, rushed ahead of the Spirit or strayed away from the narrow path. Taking a few minutes in the middle of the day, maybe even physically walking around the block with God, quietly reciting a prayer or Bible verse, will be sustaining. We will often find our perspective return, our day re-orientated and ourselves back in step with God.

I love the 'None' (ninth hour) prayers in religious houses, the gathering in the early afternoon in the monastery chapel for a liturgy of readings and prayers that rarely lasts more than 12 minutes, the refocusing that goes on there, the re-centring of lives upon God after the inevitable distractions of lunch. All this serves to re-establish us in Christ for the afternoon ahead. When I am at home and living intentionally, I will try to take a short walk in the middle of the day. Sometimes with the dog, sometimes on the way to a meeting, I walk intentionally mindful of God, 'practising the presence', as Brother Lawrence says. Sometimes I even imagine Jesus alongside. This helps me enter into a 'thin place' where I invite heaven to collide with earth. A few minutes in midday communion like this and we regain a sense of God's kingdom which has during the course of the morning become hidden from view. My small issues and local problems always look different after time spent intentionally walking with God, seen through his eternal omniscient eyes. The spirit of this age, I am reminded, has been overcome and I remember that I am once again secure, loved by one who is before, over and beyond all time and space.

Creating rhythms of daily prayer around watching, waiting and walking will come more easily for some than others, but they are habits that changed Peter, and I believe these disciplines have featured under different names in many believers' lives. Moving daily through each of them will provide a scaffold not just for our prayer but for our whole life. God wants us to slide easily in and out of daily communion with him. He rejoices when we overcome the struggle and enter that place weary. He longs for us to turn to him. By shaping the day we will find ourselves developing habitual patterns of turning to him in confession, in contemplation and in the rhythmic moments of communion as we walk with him each day. What brings him sadness is when his children turn away or ignore the offer of his enduring loving presence.

Just as each of us has a personal gait, so we will each need to find the exact shape and pattern of daily prayer that suits us best. Some have more time in the morning than the evening, some find contemplation difficult and need only a few minutes to be restored. Our personalities and lifestyle need to be borne in mind as we develop our own patterns around these three holy habits. As we adopt the holy habits they will in turn shape our personality and lifestyle and we will sense transformation occurring within us; we may become as naturally prayerful as the saints who inspire us.

If in our desire to walk more closely with God we want to shape our days most effectively, there are some basic questions we should ask:

- *What sort of a walker am I?* Do I live life in small chunks or do I prefer longer periods of concentration? One person will appreciate three or four times of short Godward focus during the day, while another, like Martin Luther, may find two or three hours of prayer at the start of each day to be the best rhythm.
- *When do I enjoy walking most?* Am I an evening or a morning person? Most of us tend to use the best time of our day to catch up with emails or to squeeze in extra time for work or the gym. Coming to God with scraps of time, we can barely focus on him and quickly lose interest in our prayers – quite the opposite of the call of Scripture to tithe God our first fruits, our best time. Prayer will always be more fulfilling if we come to it awake and engaged.
- *How do the habits fit best with my other daily activities?* When am I busy and when am I reflective and when do I need to be elsewhere? To use the three holy habits really well on a daily basis we need to listen to our own body clock. Trying to be still when our bodies are most active may be unwise; coffee before contemplation may not work for some of us!

Our patterns will be unique. A friend of mine likes to settle down with God late at night for an hour or so; he is an owl and not a lark and can best give himself to God then. A young mum I know was struggling to find more than five minutes away from her small child, so she now has five or six rich mini-moments a day with a memory verse instead of feeling guilty about not finding half an hour for God at a stretch. Married friends of mine take time out on Saturday morning for couple or family prayers which form the cornerstone for shorter times of individual prayer during the week. I have a monthly pattern of 'first thing' verses that I read each morning to anchor my day before anything else can get in!

God is the same yesterday, today and for ever. Millions of people for thousands of years in hundreds of ways have learnt to lean into God. There is no one right way, but there is a 'better way'. As Jesus explained to Martha, it involves stopping, resisting the lure of the world, the distractions of the immediate, the addictive lure of busyness and the list of jobs, and *wasting time in prayer* hanging out gladly with Jesus.

6

Holy habits along life's path

————◆·◆·◆————

> There is a time for everything, and a season for
> every activity under the heavens.
>
> (Ecclesiastes 3.1)

Practising the habits within a daily routine is a great way to build them into our lives, but there is also a real value in using them more widely through the seasons and chapters of our lives; the seasons and chapters that comprise the path we are seeking to walk with God.

We often think the Bible starts in Eden, but it actually starts 'In the beginning, God' – and then records the chronology of creation. God pre-exists creation. Day and night were his idea and the sun and moon were made by him. On the third day he made the seasons, to give the earth a natural pattern of birth, decay and new birth. By the end of creation we see that God liked the idea of a week, something he reinforces in his commandments by giving us one complete day of rest in every seven. If we lived as he intended, our lives would be generally more healthy and life-giving. Once we have found daily rhythms for drawing near to God, we should take cognisance of these other natural rhythms and seasons, and learn to live with them.

Most of us live life in weeks: work days, weekends and Thursday nights out – our lives acknowledge the pattern of the week without us thinking much about it. Appointments at the doctor's are often measured this way – 'Come back in a week or two if nothing changes'. All this is drawn from a story that many don't believe in, but the pattern is here to stay despite the seven-day shopping frenzy and the 24/7 lives of bankers and the internet. We are unlikely to have patterns of prayer that don't in some way follow the shape of the week. There is simply more time on certain days, while other days have more structure. Living the week, we can enjoy the pattern rather than trying to force another routine on to it. I like using the creation chronology to shape my prayers; I enjoy having more time on my day off to walk the dog intentionally in God's presence. The more structured days (I try not to describe them as busy before I get there) lend themselves well to a more structured pattern of morning and evening prayers, and it is harder to put time into the middle of them to check my step.

The seasons of the year will also work against us if we don't work with them. My grandfather was a farmer: growing up, I heard stories of how the church bells would call farm staff to down tools in the field to pray, and I observed for myself country churches with no electric light moving the time of evening worship so that worshippers could meet in the daylight. Simply having longer days with better light lifts the mood for many, and they also allow us to get out and about more often so that walking becomes a pleasure and can take place later into the evening. The winter days when the home is cold first thing do not invite us to sit still for too long. But dark early evenings with central heating, sitting in confession or contemplation, seem less of a rush.

Each year we move through a longer cycle, for there are some things we do just once a year: birthdays, Christmas, Easter, going on holiday and maybe taking a retreat to review our life's course. The Christian festivals are often taken over by secularity; we would do well to consider how our personal walk with God can claim them back and use them as markers along life's path. *Time to Pray* is a handy Church of England publication that does just this, giving daily readings, canticles and psalms for the seasons.[18] The late John Stott would share his routine with young Christians: an hour a day, a day a month, a week a year, periods of retreat and review built into the natural flow of the year. Not all of us can easily find a day a month to be still and know God, but many of us could use some of our annual leave for a retreat. Taking a retreat may be new for some, but I would urge us all to try it once and see if God uses it to meet with us or teach us something new. One treat of the retreat is being away from responsibilities and dependants; switching off the phone we can live our daily rhythms with less interruption, and if in a religious house we can share and rejoice in the rhythms of others.

As well as living our lives in weeks and seasons, we live in chapters. There are two types of chapter, the first being the natural chapters brought about by the ageing process and the second being triggered by events. The ageing process brings with it changing responsibilities at work and at home; for some it involves marriage and parenthood, and for all it will come to a point when instead of being minors who are cared for we become those who care for our parents. The very ageing process itself leaves us with varying amounts of energy and sleep requirements along the way. To ignore these and believe that our prayer patterns can be the same over more than six or seven years is to miss completely something of the beauty and design that God has poured into his creation of humanity. To work with the ageing process is to enjoy the new opportunities at every stage rather than trying to cling to the past, and as we do this in our patterns of prayer we will find other areas of our life transformed. God loves that.

The second form of chapter that we live through is the event-triggered chapters. The loss of a job, the finding of a partner, moving home or losing a friend or parent, all impact our lives. To live as though they don't affect us will leave us with buried grief, conflicted dreams and psychosomatic symptoms. Any but the newest of believers knows that the Christian life is not constantly alongside streams of living water: we also pass through shadow lands, stormy seas and arid deserts. These are often unexpected, and we realize 18 months later that we have been moving slowly through a fog of feelings that have permeated our whole being. We must constantly ask God for the gift of

discernment, which can help us grow in both self-awareness and other-awareness. Discerning the chapter we are in and its impact on us will be a real aid to our being set free to address both the joys and the pain it is causing, to seek any healing that we need and then to enjoy the growth that God is bringing about.

The three holy habits are a way of looking at where we have come to. Are we naturally in watching mode? Why? Are we finding ourselves unable to wait on God? What is the root cause of that? Are we walking with God or walking too often alone or with some other spiritual influence? We can also make choices about the seasons we feel or are being encouraged to enter. After a bereavement we may need to wait on God for a season, unable to focus clearly enough to do the watching and too weary to walk confidently in his light. After a mistake or a period of failure we would do well to take a season of watching in order to 'watch and pray' that we might not again fall into temptation. These can become for us spiritual seasons with which to understand our life and to live it well.

Many Christians have discovered the joy of journalling: keeping a spiritual diary or log book, tracing the changes and chapters of the spiritual journey. My own are always well-chosen hard-back books of plain unlined paper. They include prayers I have written, pictures I have drawn or taken with a camera, letters to God, personal notes and revisions to my rule of life. My journal accompanies me on quiet days and into retreat; some days I grab it to put in an entry during my time of morning prayer. I don't often read back through the pages and sometimes I don't go to my journal for weeks. Whenever I fill a book, I always keep it safe with my other old full journals. If those of us who keep journals take time to look back through them, we will often perceive spiritual seasons and chapters we were barely aware of at the time.

A season of watching may need to be entered, as mentioned above, to resolve some deep inner questions or uncertainty. It may be forced upon us and we may simply find ourselves watching and wondering how on earth life has brought us to

this place. Many choose to enter a season of watching each Lent. A season of reflection, confession and learning will generally be a time of preparation, tilling the soil of our lives to bring back vitality or to prepare it for new seeds of growth. This season might be marked by preparing for and going on retreat, or choosing, if we are able, to take a sabbatical. It may be that we simply set aside a few weeks or months in daily life to come before God in an attitude of watching, perhaps seeking his direction in some life decision. We should not seek to stay in the season of watching too long, though, for some personality types will become comfortable, secure and over-introspective. God calls us to reach out, to live beyond ourselves; we retreat to go forward. For most of us, if this season includes good times of personal reflection and a rich consideration of our doctrine, it will move us towards him in worship and adoration.

A season of waiting is sometimes entered through worship and adoration. It often happens at the times in our life when we know the next step but not God's timing – we are quite literally in the waiting room. We may be waiting for an opening with our work or ministry; we know change is coming and are prepared. We need, to be sure, to wait on God, to seek his Holy Spirit just as the disciples did. It could be we are waiting with terminal illness – our own or that of others. We wait on God for his timing and delivery and for his Spirit to take those left behind through the shadow lands. We wait at the bus stop to visit, we wait in the waiting room for the doctors to finish their rounds, waiting has come upon us; whether the season is chosen or not chosen, we are wise to recognize it and wait on God, for without him we can do nothing. Again, we may choose to go on retreat in order to wait more intentionally, or if it is a season that we find ourselves in we will more probably need to adjust our daily and weekly routines to provide more opportunity for this aspect of our prayer.

These waiting seasons are a little like a plant waiting in the ground, often preceding something new: growth, responsibility, ministry, relationship or adventures. It is easy to be frustrated when

a season like this comes upon us; we are naturally impatient. But as Sarah, Moses, Mary, the disciples and countless others have discovered, God's word is true; 'Blessed are those who listen to me, watching daily at my doors, waiting at my doorway. For those who find me find life, and receive favour from the LORD' (Proverbs 8.34–35). Too often this season gets overlooked or bypassed and we miss out on all that God wants to grow in us by way of patience and faith.

There is an obvious biblical season we should all observe. From Ascension Day to Pentecost, I suggest we 'wait on God' as we journey with the disciples through the ten days of Ascensiontide, consciously opening ourselves to grow in patience, expectation and faith, waiting day after day for his Spirit to fill us. We might precede this during the 40 days of Eastertide, watching over our life and doctrine in the light of the cross and Resurrection. I don't use Lent much myself but it can be a time to practise living – not six weeks of austerity but a season to review our disciplines. But we are Easter people and we ought to live in the light of Easter and the power of the Spirit. Let us return each Easter to a season of watching and move into waiting for the ten days leading to Pentecost, leaning and looking into God for more of him in our lives.

Walking with God is not really a season. Rather, it is, to use the title of a well-known book, the 'normal Christian life'. This should be where we spend most of our time while daily and weekly cultivating the other two habits. It is the place that hopefully we increasingly find ourselves and to which we aspire to return whenever we are watching or waiting with God. From time to time we will need to check our stride more fully than we can in the daily round. We will need to pause along the way to drink from the river of life so that, fortified, we may go on. It is a mistake to believe we can live healthy transformed lives without doing this. My quiet days I now call 'faith and purpose days'; I split the time between reflecting on my journey of faith and considering my ministry and purpose. I take them periodically throughout the year and often draw a theme from a nearby saint's day, such as St Paul in January or St Cuthbert in March. I almost always return home refreshed and with new perspective, quite literally with a spring in my step.

Between the seasons and chapters forced upon us or chosen lie times of transition. Some love transition and some hate it, but many of these chapter or seasonal transitions are only realized when we look backwards. Quiet days and retreats can really help us with transitional moments. Time spent with a spiritual director or going to a conference can also ensure the transition is marked and healthy. Habits around quiet days can help us spot the transitional stages we have hitherto ignored. Many of us are rubbish at transition. It is as if we have tripped and hurt our ankle but think we can walk exactly as before. The opposite is true, and we will walk with a limp, ending the day in pain quite out of proportion with the original fall. Of course, Jacob comes to mind, walking with a limp after wrestling with God all night. Sometimes God allows us to trip because he wants us to change our gait: he wants to help us into a new spiritual awakening. 'Be alert and of sober mind so that you may pray,' Peter says (1 Peter 4.7).

'Take time to smell the flowers' is a phrase that has stuck in my mind; slowing down we gain perspective, smelling the flowers we know the season. God will help us through these step changes, for nothing is impossible for him and he longs to be with us in the good times, the bad times and the times in between.

We might at these transitional points want to ask ourselves:

1 What season am I in? Is the winter affecting my mood? Am I still grieving? Is my life situation new and not yet fully embraced?

2 Is it time to change seasons? Have I been walking for a long time with no real rest and refreshment?

3 To which season is God calling me right now? Do I need to take time for reflection or being still?

The psalmist says to God, 'All the days ordained for me were written in your book before one of them came to be' (Psalm 139.16). Isn't it odd that we so often leave God out of the picture?

I don't mean that we stop praying or going to church – we may even sing to him as we walk down the street – but we have stopped seeking him for who he is. If God knows us better than we do ourselves, it may be that he knows which season we are in before we even realize the change. It may be a while since you asked God to help you pray! Again the psalmist declares, 'You make known to me the path of life; you will fill me with joy in your presence, with eternal pleasures at your right hand' (Psalm 16.11). May we each let God in a little further: he knows the plans he has for us and the path he wants us to walk with him.

If we are not seeking God for his guidance in our very relationship with him it is time for a new season, one of watching to reflect on the obstinacy within ourselves and confess it, to consider why we have turned away from his grace, love, power and presence. We need to return to our first habit. And once we have been there a while we need to be still and know God afresh in our second habit. Then we can come again into the light of his love with our third and most important habit, walking with God.

I believe Peter learnt to watch his life and consider theologically his friend and Saviour. Through waiting, he discovered the rich gift of God's unlimited divine power and, through receiving the Holy Spirit, he walked with God in a way that would bring others to the same rhythmic way of life.

> Yes, LORD, walking in the way of your laws,
> we wait for you;
> your name and renown
> are the desire of our hearts.
> My soul yearns for you in the night;
> in the morning my spirit longs for you.
>   (Isaiah 26.8–9a)

> Let us walk in His paths by the guidance of the
> Gospel that we may deserve to see Him who
>   has called us to His kingdom.
>   (St Benedict)[19]

Notes

1 Andy Rider, *Three Holy Habits* (Cambridge: Grove Books, 2009), p. 16.
2 G. Wakefield, *A Dictionary of Christian Spirituality* (London: SCM Press, 1983), p. 341.
3 *The Rule of St Benedict* (London: Vintage, 1998), Prologue.
4 Watchman Nee, *Sit, Walk, Stand*, fourth edition (Wheaton, IL: Tyndale, 1977), p. 14.
5 David Runcorn is a writer, theological educator and spiritual director; he has kept chickens and has helped many to find God in more places than they imagined.
6 The 'religious life' is the term given to the way of life of those who have taken religious vows and entered an order, most notably monks and nuns and most often to be found living in a 'religious house', a community of people with a common set of vows and a common life.
7 Bernard of Clairvaux, Sermon 18: 'The Two Operations of the Holy Spirit', *Sermons on the Song of Songs*.
8 Rider, *Three Holy Habits*, p. 16.
9 Andrew Murray, *Waiting on God* (New Kensington, PA: Whitaker House, 1981).
10 Rider, *Three Holy Habits*.
11 Paula Gooder, *The Meaning is in the Waiting* (Norwich: Canterbury Press, 2006), p. 6.
12 This I believe is the prayer Jesus prays in Gethsemane, the prayer, 'Father, thy will be done.'
13 Thomas Merton, *What is Contemplation?*, tenth edition (Springfield, IL: Templegate, 1950), p. 11.
14 Brother Lawrence, *The Practice of the Presence of God* (Radford, VA: Wilder, 2008), Second Letter.
15 Rider, *Three Holy Habits*, p. 20.
16 Brother Lawrence, *Practice*, Fifth Letter.
17 W. W. Simpson, *Jewish Prayer and Worship: An introduction for Christians* (London: SCM Press, 2012; originally published 1965).
18 *Time to Pray* (London: Church House Publishing, 2006).
19 *Rule of St Benedict*, Prologue, p. 21.

ND - #0059 - 270325 - C0 - 198/129/7 - PB - 9780281063949 - Matt Lamination